Fodors P

buqqpest

Excerpted from *Fodor's Eastern and Central Europe*
fodor's travel publications
new york · toronto · london · sydney · auckland
www.fodors.com

contents

maps

ON THE ROAD WITH FODOR'S

EVERY TRIP IS A SIGNIFICANT TRIP. Acutely aware of that fact, we've pulled out all stops in preparing Fodor's *Pocket Budapest*. To guide you in putting together your Budapest experience, we've created multiday itineraries and regional tours. And to direct you to the places that are truly worth your time and money, we've rallied the team of endearingly picky know-it-alls we're pleased to call our writers. Having seen all corners of Budapest, they're real experts. If you knew them, you'd poll them for tips yourself.

Betsy Maury, a former senior editor with the U.S. publisher Bantam Doubleday Dell, spent four years in Slovenia before settling in Budapest, where she now lives with her husband and works as a freelance writer. She updated the Budapest dining and lodging reviews for our guide.

Upon receiving an MA in writing in 1990, **Paul Olchváry,** a western New York native, moved to the land of his ancestors, Hungary, expecting to stay a year or so. He stayed for ten. Initially a university composition instructor, he went on to hold a fellowship at the U.S. Embassy in Budapest before becoming founding editor of an English-language digest of Hungarian news. From the mid-1990s on, he focused on his own writing, literary translation, and copyediting. In addition to updating our Hungary chapter, he has published numerous stories and essays, many in Hungarian translation, and written three novels, two of them set in present-day Hungary. He has also rendered seven books and numerous shorter works from Hungarian to English.

We would like to thank Malév Hungarian Airlines for its help with realizing this book.

Don't Forget to Write

Keeping a travel guide fresh and up-to-date is a big job. So we love your feedback—positive and negative—and follow up on all suggestions. Contact the Budapest editor at editors@fodors.com or c/o Fodor's, 280 Park Avenue, New York, NY 10017. And have a wonderful trip!

Karen Cure

Karen Cure
Editorial Director

ÓBUDA

Margit-sziget
(Margaret Is.)

Margithíd
(Margaret Br.)

Katona József u.

Rómer Flóris u.

Frankel Leó út

Mártírok útja

Szent István körút

Pannónia u.

Balaton u.

Bem József u.

Margit körút

Bem rakpart

Fő u.

Kacsa u.

Varsányi Irén u.

Csalogány u.

Markó u.

Szemere u.

Kossuth
Lajos tér

Moszkva
tér

Batthyány u.

Alkotmány u.

Szabadság
tér

Báthori u.

Bem rakpart

Donáti u.

Toldy Ferenc u.

Szabó Ilonka u.

Táncsics u. M. u.

Fortuna u.

Úri utca

Országház u.

Tóth Árpád sétány

Lovas

Hunyadi János út

Zoltán u.

Szabadság
tér

Danube

Széchenyi rakpart

Arany János u.

Nádor u.

Várhegy

Fő u.

BUDA

PEST

Vérmező

Logodi u.

sétány

Dísz
tér

Roosevelt
tér

Clark
Ádám
tér

Széchenyi
lánchíd
(Chain Br.)

József Attila u.

Déli pu.
(South
Station)

Attila út

Erzsébet
tér

Belgrád

Alagút u.

Na phegy

Krisztina körút

Lisznyay u.

Groza P. rakpart

Vörösmarty
tér

Váci utca

Petőfi Sándor u.

Deák F. u.

Avar u.

Mészáros u.

Tigris u.

Tabán

Ferenc
tere

Csörsz u.

Hegyalja út

Hegyalja út

Orom u.

Döbrentei
tér

Alsó hegy u.

Bérc u.

Ször les. u.

Erzsébethíd
(Elizabeth Br.)

Szt. Gellért rakpart

Somlói út

Kelenhegyi út

Gellért
Hill

Szent
Gellért
tér

Kelenhegyi út

Alsóhegy u.

Villányi út

Ménesi út

Somlói út

← TO SZOBOR PARK

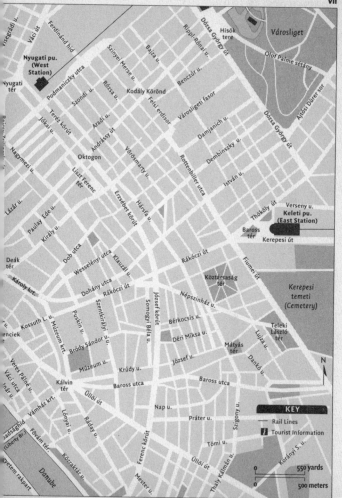

Váci út
Ferdinánd híd
Visegrádi u.
Dózsa György út
Rippl-Rónai u.
Hősök tere
Városliget
Nyugati pu. (West Station)
Szinyei Merse u.
Bajza u.
Olof Palme sétány
Nyugati tér
Podmaniczky utca
Benczúr u.
Szondi u.
Rózsa u.
Kodály Körönd
Teréz körút
Aradi u.
Andrássy út
Feisl erdősor
Városligeti fasor
Damjanich u.
Ajtósi Dürer sor
Dózsa György út
Jókai u.
Nagymező u.
Oktogon
Vörösmarty u.
Dembinszky u.
Liszt Ferenc tér
Erzsébet körút
Rottenbiller utca
István u.
Lázár u.
Hársfa u.
Thököly út
Verseny u.
Keleti pu. (East Station)
Paulay Ede u.
Baross tér
Király u.
Dob utca
Wesselényi utca
Klauzál u.
Kerepesi út
Deák tér
Károly krt.
Dohány utca
Rákóczi út
Rákóczi út
Fiumei út
Köztársaság tér
Kerepesi temeti (Cemetery)
Kossuth L. u.
Múzeum krt.
Puskin u.
Szentkirály
Somogyi Béla u.
József körút
Népszinház u.
Bérkocsis u.
Teleki László tér
Lujza u.
Bródy Sándor u.
Déri Miksa u.
Mátyás tér
Dankó u.
Ferenciek
Veres Pálné u.
Váci utca
Múzeum u.
Krúdy u.
József u.
Kálvin tér
Baross utca
Baross utca
Szabadsághíd (Liberty Br.)
Vámház krt.
Lónyai u.
Üllői út
Nap u.
Práter u.
Szigony u.
N
Egyetem rakpart
Fővám tér
Ráday u.
Ferenc körút
Tömi u.
Thály Kálmán u.
Korányi S. u.
Közraktár u.
Mester u.
Üllői út
Danube

KEY
— Rail Lines
🄸 Tourist Information

0 — 550 yards
0 — 500 meters

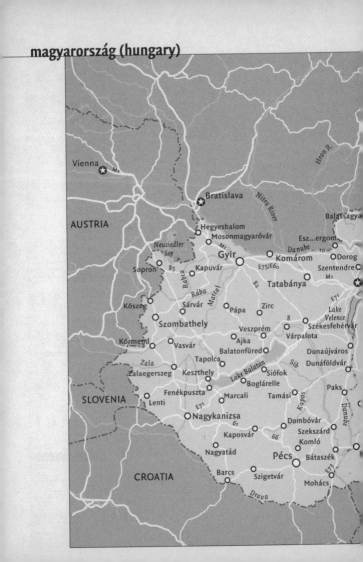

budapest

In This Chapter

Updated by Julie Tomasz

introducing
budapest

SITUATED ON BOTH BANKS of the Danube, Budapest unites the colorful hills of Buda and the wide, businesslike boulevards of Pest. Though it was the site of a Roman outpost during the 1st century, the city was not officially created until 1873, when the towns of Óbuda, Pest, and Buda were joined. Since then, Budapest has been the cultural, political, intellectual, and commercial heart of Hungary; for the 20% of the nation's population who live in the capital, anywhere else is simply *vidék* ("the country").

Budapest has suffered many ravages in the course of its long history. It was totally destroyed by the Mongols in 1241, captured by the Turks in 1541, and nearly destroyed again by Soviet troops in 1945. But this bustling industrial and cultural center survived as the capital of the People's Republic of Hungary after the war—and then, as the 1980s drew to a close, it became one of the Eastern Bloc's few thriving bastions of capitalism. Today, judging by the city's flourishing cafés and restaurants, markets and bars, the stagnation enforced by the Communists seems a thing of the very distant past.

Much of the charm of a visit to Budapest lies in unexpected glimpses into shadowy courtyards and in long vistas down sunlit cobbled streets. Although some 30,000 buildings were destroyed during World War II and in 1956, the past lingers on in the often crumbling architectural details of the antique structures that remain.

NEW AND NOTEWORTHY

Grand old **Budapest** is seeing more and more development, from private restoration of crumbling buildings to city-funded projects, such as the increase in pedestrian-only zones. Political tensions between the governments of capital and country may have stalled construction of a new National Theater and a fourth metro line, but Hungary's overall stability and continued attraction of foreign investment have fostered ongoing revitalization. Indeed, theater and café culture seems no worse for politics. While many Hungarians can hardly afford to go out to eat, an emerging middle class has gradually instilled Budapest with confidence unseen since the heady days of the Austro-Hungarian empire a century ago.

Slowly but surely, Hungary continues to **improve its infrastructure,** helping it fill its increasingly important role as a link between Eastern and Western Europe. Over the next several years, major highways will continue to be upgraded and extended, and the airport in Budapest has seen major expansion in the past few years. Last but not least, the once-antiquated telephone system is being overhauled. While progress is apparent, travelers should note that in Hungary, silence at the other end of the line is still assumed to be a broken connection rather than a crank call.

At press time, Hungary's annual inflation rate had dropped under 10% from the 25% of five years earlier, and with continued significant devaluation of the forint, exchange rates keep improving for visitors from North America and Great Britain. Yet, while Hungary remains a bargain compared to Western Europe, strictly rock-bottom prices are a thing of the past.

PLEASURES AND PASTIMES

DINING

Through the lean postwar years the Hungarian kitchen lost none of its spice and sparkle. Meats, rich sauces, and creamy desserts predominate, but the more health-conscious will also find salads, even out of season. (Strict vegetarians should note, however, that even meatless dishes are usually cooked with lard [zsír].) In addition to the ubiquitous dishes with which most foreigners are familiar, such as chunky beef gulyás (goulash) and paprikás csirke (chicken paprika) served with galuska (little pinched dumplings), traditional Hungarian classics include fiery halászlé (fish soup), scarlet with hot paprika; fogas (pike perch) from Lake Balaton; and goose liver, duck, and veal specialties. Lake Balaton is the major source of fish in Hungary, particularly for süllő, a kind of perch. Hungarians are also very fond of carp (ponty), catfish (harcsa), and eel (angolna), which are usually stewed in a garlic-and-tomato sauce.

Portions are large, so don't plan to eat more than one main Hungarian meal a day. Desserts are lavish, and every inn seems to have its house torta (cake), though rétes (strudels), Somlói galuska (a steamed sponge cake soaked in chocolate sauce and whipped cream), and palacsinta (stuffed crepes) are ubiquitous. Traditional rétes fillings are mák (sugary poppy seeds), meggy (sour cherry), and túró (sweetened cottage cheese); palacsintas always come rolled with dió (sweet ground walnuts), túró, or lekvár (jam)—usually barack (apricot).

FOLK ART

Hungary's centuries-old traditions of handmade, often regionally specific folk art are still beautifully alive. Intricately carved wooden boxes, vibrantly colorful embroidered tablecloths and shirts, matte-black pottery pitchers, delicately woven lace collars, ceramic plates splashed with painted flowers and birds, and decorative heavy leather whips are among the favorite handcrafted pieces a visitor can purchase. You can purchase them directly from the artisans at crafts fairs and from peddlers on the streets. Dolls dressed in national costume are also popular souvenirs.

LODGING

Many of the major luxury and business-class hotel chains are represented in Budapest; however, all of them are Hungarian-run franchise operations with native touches that you won't find in any other Hilton or Marriott. Guest houses, also called *panziók* (pensions), provide simple accommodations—well suited to people on a budget. Like B&Bs, most are run by couples or families and offer simple breakfast facilities and usually have private bathrooms; they're generally outside the city or town center. Arrangements can be made directly with the panzió or through local tourist offices and travel agents abroad. Another good budget option is renting a room in a private home. Reservations and referrals can also be made by any tourist office.

PORCELAIN

Among the most sought-after items in Hungary are the exquisite hand-painted Herend and Zsolnay porcelain. Unfortunately, the prices on all makes of porcelain have risen considerably in the last few years. For guaranteed authenticity, make your purchases at the Herend and Zsolnay stores in Budapest.

SPAS AND THERMAL BATHS

Several thousand years ago, the first settlers of the area that is now Budapest chose their home because of its abundance of hot springs. Centuries later, the Romans and the Turks built baths and developed cultures based on medicinal bathing. Now there are more than 1,000 medicinal hot springs bubbling up around the country. Budapest alone has some 14 historic working baths, which attract ailing patients with medical prescriptions for specific water cures as well as "recreational" bathers—locals and tourists alike—wanting to soak in the relaxing waters, try some of the many massages and treatments, and experience the architectural beauty of the bathhouses themselves.

For most, a visit to a bath involves soaking in several thermal pools of varying temperatures and curative contents—perhaps throwing in a game of aquatic chess—relaxing in a steam room or sauna, and getting a brisk, if not brutal, massage (average cost: 200 Ft. for a half hour). Many bath facilities are single-sex or have certain days set aside for men or women only, and most people walk around nude or with miniature loincloths, provided at the door. Men should be aware that some men-only baths have a strong gay clientele.

In addition to the ancient beauties there are newer, modern baths open to the public at many spa hotels. They lack the charm and aesthetic appeal of their older peers but provide the latest treatments in sparkling facilities. For more information, page through the "Hungary: Land of Spas" brochure published by the Hungarian Tourist Board, available free from most tourist offices.

WINE, BEER, AND SPIRITS

Hungary tempts wine connoisseurs with its important wine regions, especially Villány, near Pécs, in the south; Eger and Tokaj in the north; and the northern shore of Lake Balaton.

Kéknyelű, Szürkebarát, and especially Olaszrizling are all common white table wines; Tokay, one of the great wines of the world, can be heavy, dark, and sweet, and is generally drunk as an aperitif or a dessert wine. It's expensive, especially by Hungarian standards, so it's usually reserved for special occasions. The gourmet red table wine of Hungary, Egri Bikavér (Bull's Blood of Eger, usually with el toro himself on the label), is the best buy and the safest bet with all foods.

Before- and after-dinner drinks tend toward schnapps, most notably Barack-pálinka, an apricot brandy. A plum brandy called Kosher szilva-pálinka, bottled under rabbinical supervision, is very chic. Unicum, Hungary's national liqueur, is a dark, thick, vaguely minty, and quite potent drink that could be likened to

Germany's Jägermeister. Its chubby green bottle makes it a good souvenir to take home.

Major Hungarian beers are Köbányai, Dreher, Aranyhordó, Balaton Világos, and Aszok.

QUICK TOURS

If you're here for just a short period you need to plan carefully so as to make the most of your time in Budapest. The following itineraries outline major sights throughout the city, and will help you structure your visit efficiently. Each is intended to take about four hours—a perfect way to fill a free morning or afternoon. For more information about individual sights, *see* Here and There.

VÁRHEGY (CASTLE HILL)

Buda's **Várhegy** district is a must-see on even the shortest itinerary. Spend the day strolling its cobblestone streets, stopping to view exhibits at the **Nemzeti Galéria** (National Gallery) or any other museum in the **Királyi palota** (Royal Palace) complex. After visiting the magnificent **Mátyás templom** (Matthias Church), walk behind it to the **Halászbástya** (Fisherman's Bastion) and indulge in the postcard Danube views framed in the Halászbástya's cheerful white stone arches.

SIGHTS AND SOAKS: BUDA

Climb the winding foot path to the top of **Gellért Hill** (roughly a half-hour walk), stopping for a close-up view of the massive **Szabadság szobor** (Liberation Monument) that presides over the Danube's Buda bank. Stroll along the stone walls of the **Citadella**, taking in the sweeping vistas over the Danube and Pest. Hike back down to the foot of the hill and reward your efforts with a therapeutic soak in the ornate thermal baths of Hungary's most famous spa hotel, the **Gellért Hotel.**

SIGHTS AND SOAKS: PEST

Start at **Hősök tere** (Heroes' Square), taking in exhibits at the **Szépművészeti Múzeum** (Museum of Fine Arts) and/or the **Műcsarnok** (Palace of Exhibitions), strolling through the grounds of the **Vajdahunyad Vár** (Vajdahunyad Castle), then walking farther into **Városliget** (City Park) to the elegant old **Széchenyi Fürdő** (Széchenyi Baths), where you can end your tour in any of its warm bubbling pools.

✓ VÁCI UTCA AND THE DANUBE

A leisurely few hours of strolling and shopping can begin with a pastry and espresso at Gerbeaud on **Vörösmarty tér.** From here, you can walk out to the **Korsó** and promenade along the Danube for quintessential views of Castle and Gellért hills. Double back to Vörösmarty tér and make your way down Budapest's most touristy street, **Váci utca,** a pedestrian-only zone lined with souvenir shops and expensive boutiques. At the downriver end of Váci utca is the cavernous **Vásárcsarnok** (Central Market Hall), where you can browse through dried paprika chains and salamis.

ANDRÁSSY ÚT AND THE OPERAHÁZ (OPERA HOUSE)

Start by visiting the **Szent István Bazilika** (St. Stephen's Basilica) and the **Nagy Zsinagóga** (Great Synagogue), about a 10-minute walk from each other. Then head over to the base of **Andrássy út** and begin walking to its other end, at **Hősök tere.** Without any pauses, the walk would take about 45 minutes, but you'll want to stop along the way—to admire the **Operaház** (Opera House) and to have a cappuccino at the **Művész** café, whose outdoor tables are perfect for people-watching. If you're interested in taking a 50-minute guided tour of the Opera House, plan on arriving around 3 or 4 PM. At Heroes' Square, you can visit both the **Szépművészeti Múzeum** and the **Műcsarnok.**

In This Chapter

Updated by Paul Olchváry

here and there

THE PRINCIPAL SIGHTS of Budapest fall roughly into three areas, each of which can be comfortably covered on foot. The Budapest hills are best explored by public transportation. Note that street names have changed in the past several years to purge all reminders of the Communist regime. Also note that a Roman-numeral prefix listed before an address refers to one of Budapest's 22 districts.

✓ VÁRHEGY (CASTLE HILL)

Most of the major sights of Buda are on Várhegy (Castle Hill), a long, narrow plateau laced with cobblestone streets, clustered with beautifully preserved Baroque, Gothic, and Renaissance houses, and crowned by the magnificent Royal Palace. The area is theoretically banned to private cars (except for those of neighborhood residents and Hilton Hotel guests), but the streets manage to be lined bumper to bumper with Trabants and Mercedes all the same—sometimes the only visual element to verify you're not in a fairy tale. As in all of Budapest, thriving urban new has taken up residence in historic old; international corporate offices, diplomatic residences, restaurants, and boutiques occupy many of its landmark buildings. But these are still the exceptions, as families occupy most flats and homes. ✓ The most striking example, perhaps, is the Hilton Hotel on Hess András tér, which has ingeniously incorporated remains of Castle Hill's oldest church (a tower and one wall), built by Dominican friars in the 13th century.

Numbers in the text correspond to numbers in the margin and on the Várhegy (Castle Hill) map.

várhegy (castle hill)

A Good Walk

Castle Hill's cobblestone streets and numerous museums are made to be explored on foot: Plan to spend about a day here. Most of the transportation options for getting to Castle Hill deposit you on Szent György tér or Dísz tér. It's impossible not to find Castle Hill, but it is possible to be confused about how to get on top of it. If you're already on the Buda side of the river, you can take the Castle bus—*Várbusz*—from the Moszkva tér metro station, northwest of Castle Hill. If you're starting out from Pest, you can take a taxi or Bus 16 from Erzsébet tér or, the most scenic alternative, cross the Széchenyi Lánchíd (Chain Bridge) on foot to Clark Ádám tér and ride the Sikló (funicular) up Castle Hill (☞ Clark Ádám tér, *below*).

Begin your exploration by walking slightly farther south to visit the **Királyi Palota** at the southern end of the hill. Of the palace's several major museums, the **Magyar Nemzeti Galéria** ② and the **Budapesti Történeti Múzeum** ③ are particularly interesting. From here, you can cover the rest of the area by walking north along its handful of cobbled streets. From Dísz tér, start with Tárnok utca, whose houses and usually open courtyards offer glimpses of how Hungarians have integrated contemporary life into Gothic, Renaissance, and Baroque settings; of particular interest are the houses at No. 16, now the Aranyhordó restaurant, and at No. 18, the 15th-century Arany Sas Patika (Golden Eagle Pharmacy Museum), with a naïf Madonna and child in an overhead niche. This tiny museum displays instruments, prescriptions, books, and other artifacts from 16th- and 17th-century pharmacies. Modern commerce is also integrated into Tárnok utca's historic homes; you'll encounter numerous folk souvenir shops and tiny boutiques lining the street. Tárnok utca funnels into Szentháromság tér, home of **Mátyás templom** ⑤ and, just behind it, the **Halászbástya** ⑥.

After exploring them, double back to Dísz tér and set out northward again on Úri utca, which runs parallel to Tárnok utca;

this long street is lined with beautiful, genteel homes. The funny little Telefónia Museum, at No. 49, is worth a stop, as is the **Budavári Labirintus** ⑦, at No. 9. At the end of Úri utca you'll reach Kapisztrán tér. From here, you can walk south again on a parallel street, Országház utca (Parliament Street), the main thoroughfare of 18th-century Buda; it takes its name from the building at No. 28, which was the seat of Parliament from 1790 to 1807. You'll end up back at Szentháromság tér, with just two streets remaining to explore.

You can stroll down little Fortuna utca, named for the 18th-century Fortuna Inn, which now houses the **Magyar Kereskedelmi és Vendéglátóipari Múzeum** ⑧. At the end of Fortuna utca you'll reach **Bécsi kapu tér** ⑨, opening to Moszkva tér just below. Go back south on the last of the district's streets, Táncsics Mihály utca, stopping at the **Középkori Zsidó Imaház** ⑩ and the **Zenetörténeti Múzeum** ⑪. Next door, at No. 9, is the Baroque house (formerly the Royal Mint) where rebel writer Táncsics Mihály was imprisoned in the dungeons and freed by the people on the Day of Revolution, March 15, 1848. You'll find yourself in front of the Hilton Hotel, back at Hess András tér, bordering Szentháromság tér. Those whose feet haven't protested yet can finish off their tour of Castle Hill by doubling back to the northern end and strolling south back to Dísz tér on **Tóth Árpád sétány,** the romantic, tree-lined promenade along the Buda side of the hill.

TIMING

Castle Hill is small enough to cover in one day, but perusing its major museums and several tiny exhibits will require more time.

Sights to See

❾ BÉCSI KAPU TÉR (Vienna Gate Square). Marking the northern entrance to Castle Hill, the stone gateway (rebuilt in 1936) called Vienna Gate opens toward Vienna—or, closer at hand, Moszkva tér a few short blocks below. The square named after it has some fine Baroque and rococo houses but is dominated by the enormous neo-Romanesque (1913–1917) headquarters of the **Országos Levéltár** (Hungarian National Archives), which resembles a cathedral-like shrine to paperwork.

❸ BUDAPESTI TÖRTÉNETI MÚZEUM (Budapest History Museum). The palace's Baroque southern wing (E) contains the Budapest History Museum, displaying a fascinating permanent exhibit of modern Budapest history from Buda's liberation from the Turks in 1686 through the 1970s. Viewing the vintage 19th- and 20th-century photos and videos of the castle, the Széchenyi Lánchíd, and other Budapest monuments—and seeing them as the backdrop to the horrors of World War II and the 1956 Revolution—helps to put your later sightseeing in context; while you're browsing, peek out one of the windows overlooking the Danube and Pest and let it start seeping in.

Through historical documents, objects, and art, other permanent exhibits depict the medieval history of the Buda fortress and the capital as a whole. This is the best place to view remains of the medieval Royal Palace and other archaeological excavations. Some of the artifacts unearthed during excavations are in the vestibule in the basement; others are still among the remains of medieval structures. Down in the cellars are the original medieval vaults of the palace; portraits of King Matthias and his second wife, Beatrice of Aragon; and many late-14th-century statues that probably adorned the Renaissance palace. *Royal Palace (Wing E), Szt. György tér 2, tel. 1/375–7533. 400 Ft. Mar.–mid-May and mid-Sept.–Oct., Wed.–Mon. 10–6; mid-May–mid-Sept., daily 10–6; Nov.–Feb., Wed.–Mon. 10–4.*

❼ BUDAVÁRI LABIRINTUS (Labyrinth of Buda Castle). Used as a wine cellar during the 16th and 17th centuries and then as an air-raid shelter during World War II, the labyrinth—entered at Úri utca 9 below an early 18th-century house—can be explored with a tour or, if you dare, on your own. There are some English-language

(handwritten annotations:) ✓ "Outside Only." ✓ "OOO Fts"

brochures available. Úri u. 9, tel. 1/375–6858. 800 Ft. Daily 9:30–7:30.

NEED A BREAK? For a light snack, pastry, and coffee, **Café Miro** (Úri u. 30, tel. 1/375–5458) is a fresh, hip alternative to the Old World Budapest cafés.

⑫ HADTÖRTÉNETI MÚZEUM (Museum of Military History). Fittingly, this museum is lodged in a former barracks, on the northwestern corner of Kapisztrán tér. The exhibits, which include collections of uniforms and military regalia, trace the military history of Hungary from the original Magyar conquest in the 9th century through the period of Ottoman rule to the mid-20th century. You can arrange an English-language tour in advance for around 1,000 Ft. I, Tóth Árpád sétány 40, tel. 1/356–9522. 270 Ft. Apr.–Sept., Tues.–Sun. 10–6; Oct.–Mar., Tues.–Sun. 10–4.

★ **⑥ HALÁSZBÁSTYA** (Fishermen's Bastion). The wondrous porch overlooking the Danube and Pest is the neo-Romanesque Fishermen's Bastion, a merry cluster of white stone towers, arches, and columns above a modern bronze statue of St. Stephen, Hungary's first king. Medieval fishwives once peddled their wares here, but the site is now home to souvenirs, crafts, and music.

★ **KIRÁLYI PALOTA** (Royal Palace, commonly called Buda Castle). During a seven-week siege at the end of 1944, the entire Castle Hill district of palaces, mansions, and churches was turned into one vast ruin. The final German stand was in the Royal Palace, which was utterly gutted by fire; by the end of the siege its walls were reduced to rubble, and just a few scarred pillars and blackened statues protruded from the wreckage. The destruction was incalculable, yet it gave archaeologists and art historians an opportunity to discover the medieval buildings that once stood on the site of this Baroque and neo-Baroque palace. Fortunately, details of the edifices of the kings of the Árpád and Anjou dynasties, of the Holy Roman Emperor Sigismund, and of the great

15th-century king Matthias Corvinus had been preserved in some 80 medieval reports, travelogues, books, and itineraries that were subsequently used to reconstruct the complex.

The postwar rebuilding was slow and painstaking. In some places debris more than 20 ft deep had to be removed. Freed from mounds of rubble, the foundation walls and medieval castle walls were completed, and the ramparts surrounding the medieval royal residence were re-created as close to their original shape and size as possible. Out of this Herculean labor emerged the Royal Palace of today, a vast cultural center and museum complex (☞ Budapesti Történeti Múzeum, *above,* and Ludwig Múzeum, Magyar Nemzeti Galéria, *and* Országos Széchenyi Könyvtár, *below*).

⑩ KÖZÉPKORI ZSIDÓ IMAHÁZ (Medieval Synagogue). The excavated one-room Medieval Synagogue is now used as a museum. On display are objects relating to the Jewish community, including religious inscriptions, frescoes, and tombstones dating to the 15th century. *Táncsics Mihály u. 26, tel. 1/375–7533 (ext. 243). 120 Ft. May–Oct., Tues.–Fri. 10–2, weekends 10–6.*

① LUDWIG MÚZEUM. This collection of more than 200 pieces of Hungarian and contemporary international art, including works by Picasso and Lichtenstein, occupies the castle's northern wing. *Royal Palace (Wing A), Dísz tér 17, tel. 1/375–7533. 300 Ft., free Tues. Tues.–Sun. 10–6.*

⑧ MAGYAR KERESKEDELMI ÉS VENDÉGLÁTÓIPARI MÚZEUM (Hungarian Museum of Commerce and Catering). The 18th-century Fortuna Inn now serves visitors in a different way—as the Catering Museum. Displays in a permanent exhibit show the city as a tourist destination from 1870 to the 1930s; you can see, for example, what a room at the Gellért Hotel, still operating today, would have looked like in 1918. The Commerce Museum, just across the courtyard, chronicles the history of Hungarian commerce from the late 19th century to 1947, when the new, Communist regime "liberated" the economy into socialism. The four-room exhibit includes everything from an antique chocolate-and-caramel vending machine to early shoe-polish advertisements. You can rent an English-language recorded tour for 300 Ft. *Fortuna u. 4, tel. 1/ 375–6249. 120 Ft., free Fri. Wed.–Fri. 10–5, weekends 10–6.*

② MAGYAR NEMZETI GALÉRIA (Hungarian National Gallery). The immense center block of the Royal Palace (made up of Wings B, C, and D) exhibits a wide range of Hungarian fine art, from medieval ecclesiastical paintings and statues, through Gothic, Renaissance, and Baroque art, to a rich collection of 19th- and 20th-century works. Especially notable are the works of the romantic painter Mihály Munkácsy, the impressionist Pál Szinyei Merse, and the surrealist Mihály Tivadar Kosztka Csontváry, whom Picasso much admired. There is also a large collection of modern Hungarian sculpture. There are labels and commentary in English for both permanent and temporary exhibits. If you contact the museum in advance, you can book a tour for up to five people with an English-speaking guide. *Royal Palace (entrance in Wing C), Dísz tér 17, tel. 1/375–7533. Gallery 400 Ft.; tour 1,000 Ft. Mid-Mar.–Oct., Tues.–Sun. 10–6; Nov.–mid-Jan., Tues.–Sun. 10–4; mid-Jan.–mid-Mar., Tues.–Fri. 10–4, weekends 10–6).*

⑤ MÁTYÁS TEMPLOM (Matthias Church). The Gothic Matthias Church is officially the Buda Church of Our Lady but better known by the name of the 15th century's "just king" of Hungary, who was married here twice. It is sometimes called the Coronation Church, because the last two kings of Hungary were crowned here: the Hapsburg emperor Franz Joseph in 1867 and his grandnephew Karl IV in 1916. Originally built for the city's German population in the mid-13th century, the church has endured many alterations and assaults. For almost 150 years it was the main mosque of the Turkish overlords—and the predominant impact of its festive pillars is decidedly Byzantine. Badly damaged during the recapture of Buda in 1686, it was completely rebuilt between 1873 and 1896 by Frigyes Schulek, who gave it an asymmetrical western front, with one high and one low spire, and a fine rose window; the south porch is from the 14th century.

The **SZENTHÁROMSÁG KÁPOLNA** (Trinity Chapel) holds an *encolpion*, an enameled casket containing a miniature copy of the Gospel to be worn on the chest; it belonged to the 12th-century king Béla III and his wife, Anne of Chatillon. Their burial crowns and a cross, scepter, and rings found in their excavated graves are also displayed here. The church's **treasury** contains Renaissance and Baroque chalices, monstrances, and vestments. High Mass is celebrated every Sunday at 10 AM, sometimes with full orchestra and choir—and often with major soloists; get here early if you want a seat. During the summer there are usually organ recitals on Friday at 8 PM. Tourists are asked to remain at the back of the church during weddings and services (it's least intrusive to come after 9 AM weekdays and between 1 and 5 PM Sunday and holidays). I, *Szentháromság tér 2*, *tel.* 1/355–5657. *Daily 7 AM–7:30 PM. Church free, except during concerts; treasury 200 Ft. Treasury daily 9:30–5:30.*

4 **ORSZÁGOS SZÉCHENYI KÖNYVTÁR** (Széchenyi National Library). The western wing (F) of the Royal Palace is home to the National Library, which houses more than 2 million volumes. Its archives include well-preserved medieval codices, manuscripts, and historic correspondence. This is not a lending library, but the reading rooms are open to the public (though you must show a passport), and even the most valuable materials can be viewed on microfilm. Small, temporary exhibits on rare books and documents are usually on display; the hours and admission fees for these are quite variable. Note that the entire library closes for one month every summer, usually in July or August. *Royal Palace (Wing F). To arrange a tour with an English-speaking guide, tel.* 1/224–3745. *300 Ft. Reading rooms Mon.* 1–9, *Tues.–Sat.* 9–9; *exhibits Mon.* 1–6, *Tues.–Sat.* 10–6.

STATUE OF PRINCE EUGENE OF SAVOY. In front of the Royal Palace, facing the Danube by the entrance to Wing C, stands an equestrian statue of Prince Eugene of Savoy, a commander of the army that liberated Hungary from the Turks at the end of the

17th century. From here there is a superb view across the river to Pest. By entrance to Royal Palace, Wing C.

SZENTHÁROMSÁG TÉR (Holy Trinity Square). This square is named for its Baroque **Trinity Column**, erected in 1712–13 as a gesture of thanksgiving by survivors of a plague. The column stands in front of the famous Gothic Matthias Church (☞ *above*), its large pedestal a perfect seat from which to watch the wedding spectacles that take over the church on spring and summer weekends: From morning till night, frilly engaged pairs flow in one after the other and, after a brief transformation inside, back out onto the square.

★ **TÓTH ÁRPÁD SÉTÁNY** (Árpád Tóth Promenade). This romantic, tree-lined promenade along the Buda side of the hill is often mistakenly overlooked by sightseers. Beginning at the Museum of Military History (☞ *above*) the promenade takes you "behind the scenes" along the back sides of the matte-pastel Baroque houses you saw on Úri utca, with their regal arched windows and wrought-iron gates. On a late spring afternoon, the fragrance of the cherry trees and the sweeping view of the quiet Buda neighborhoods below may be enough to revive even the most weary. I, *from Kapisztrán tér to Szent György u.*

ÚRI UTCA (Úri Street). Running parallel to Tárnok utca, Úri utca has been less commercialized by boutiques and other shops; the longest and oldest street in the castle district, it is lined with many stately houses, all worth special attention for their delicately carved details. Both gateways of the Baroque palace at **Nos. 48–50** are articulated by Gothic niches. The **Telefónia Múzeum** (Telephone Museum), at No. 49, is an endearing little museum entered through a central courtyard shared with the local district police station. Although vintage telephone systems are still in use all over the country, both the oldest and most recent products of telecommunication—from the 1882 wooden box with hose attachment to the latest digital marvels—can be observed and tested here. *Telefónia Múzeum: Úri u. 49, tel. 1/201–8188. About 100 Ft. Apr.–Oct., Tues.–Sun. 10–4.*

⑪ ZENETÖRTÉNETI MÚZEUM (Museum of Music History). This handsome gray-and-pearl-stone 18th-century palace is where Beethoven allegedly stayed in 1800 when he came to Buda to conduct his works. Now a museum, it displays rare manuscripts and old instruments downstairs in its permanent collection and temporary exhibits upstairs in a small, sunlit hall. The museum also often hosts intimate classical recitals. *Táncsics Mihály u. 7, tel. 1/214–6770 (ext. 250). About 200 Ft. Mid-Nov.–late-Dec. and first 2 wks of Mar., Tues.–Sun. 10–5; mid-Mar.–mid-Nov., Tues.–Sun. 10–6.*

TABÁN AND GELLÉRT-HEGY (TABÁN AND GELLÉRT HILL)

Spreading below Castle Hill is the old quarter called Tabán (from the Turkish word for "armory"). A onetime suburb of Buda, it was known at the end of the 17th century as Little Serbia (*Rác*) because so many Serbian refugees settled here after fleeing from the Turks. It later became a district of vineyards and small taverns. Though most of the small houses characteristic of this district have been demolished—mainly in the interest of easing traffic—a few traditional buildings remain.

Gellért-hegy (Gellért Hill), 761 ft high, is the most beautiful natural formation on the Buda bank. It takes its name from St. Gellért (Gerard) of Csanad, a Venetian bishop who came to Hungary in the 11th century and, legend has it, was rolled off the top of the hill in a cart by pagans. The walk up can be tough, but take solace from the cluster of hot springs at the foot of the hill, which soothe and cure bathers at the Rác, Rudas, and Gellért baths.

Numbers in the text correspond to numbers in the margin and on the Exploring Budapest map.

A Good Walk

From the **Semmelweis Orvostörténeti Múzeum** ⑬, walk around the corner to Szarvas tér and a few yards toward the river to the **Tabán plébánia-templom** ⑭. Walking south on Attila út and crossing to the other side of Hegyalja út, you'll be at the foot of Gellért Hill. From here, take a deep breath and climb the paths and stairs to the **Citadella** ⑰ fortress at the top of the hill (about 30 minutes). After taking in the views and exploring the area, you can descend and treat yourself to a soak or a swim at the **Gellért Szálloda és Thermál Fürdő** ⑱ at the southeastern foot of the hill. On foot, take the paths down the southeastern side of the hill. You can also take Bus 27 down the back of the hill to Móricz Zsigmond körtér and walk back toward the Gellért on busy Bartók Béla út, or take Tram 47, 49, 18, or 19 a couple of stops to Szent Gellért tér.

TIMING

The Citadella and Szabadság szobor are lit in golden lights every night, but the entire Gellért-hegy is at its scenic best every year on August 20, when it forms the backdrop to the spectacular St. Stephen's Day fireworks display.

Sights to See

★ ⑰ **CITADELLA.** The fortress atop the hill was a much-hated sight for Hungarians. They called it the Gellért Bastille, for it was erected, on the site of an earlier wooden observatory, by the Austrian army as a lookout after the 1848–1849 War of Independence. But no matter what its history may be, the views here are breathtaking. Its transformation into a tourist site during the 1960s improved its image, with the addition of cafés, a beer garden, wine cellars, and a hostel. In its inner wall is a small graphic exhibition (with some relics) of Budapest's 2,000-year history. XI, Citadella sétány, No phone. Free. Fortress: daily, 24 hrs; amenities hrs vary.

✓ **ERZSÉBET HÍD** (Elizabeth Bridge). This bridge was named for Empress Elizabeth (1837–1898), called Sissi, of whom the Hungarians were particularly fond. The beautiful but unhappy wife of Franz Joseph, she was stabbed to death in 1898 by an anarchist while boarding a boat on Lake Geneva. The bridge was built between 1897 and 1903; at the time, it was the longest single-span suspension bridge in Europe.

✓ ★ ⑱ **GELLÉRT SZÁLLODA ÉS THERMÁL FÜRDŐ** (Gellért Hotel and Thermal Baths). At the foot of Gellért Hill, are these beautiful art-nouveau establishments. The Danubius Hotel Gellért (☞ Where to Stay) is the oldest spa hotel in Hungary, with hot springs that have supplied curative baths for nearly 2,000 years. It is the most popular among tourists, as you don't need reservations, it's quite easy to communicate, and there's a wealth of treatments— including chamomile steam baths, salt-vapor inhalations, and hot mud packs. Many of these treatments require a doctor's prescription; they will accept prescriptions from foreign doctors. Men and women have separate steam and sauna rooms; both the indoor pool and the outdoor wave pool (☞ Outdoor Activities and Sports) are coed. XI, Gellért tér 1, tel. 1/466–6166 (baths). Indoor baths and steam rooms 750 Ft. per 1½ hrs; indoor and pool 1,500 Ft. per day. Baths weekdays 6 AM–6 PM, weekends 6:30–4 (May–Sept. until 7). May–Sept. weekend massage only until 1 PM. Wave pool May–Sept., daily 6 AM–6 PM.

⑮ **RÁC FÜRDŐ** (Rác Baths). The bright-yellow building tucked away at the foot of Gellért Hill near the Elizabeth Bridge houses these baths, built during the reign of King Zsigmond in the early 15th century and rebuilt by Miklós Ybl in the mid-19th century. Its waters contain alkaline salts and other minerals; you can also get a massage. Women can bathe on Monday, Wednesday, and Friday; men on Tuesday, Thursday, and Saturday (☞ Outdoor Activities and Sports). These baths are particularly popular with the gay community. I, Hadnagy u. 8–10, tel. 1/356–1322. 550 Ft. Mon.–Sat. 6:30–6.

16 RUDAS FÜRDŐ (Rudas Baths). This bath is on the riverbank, the original Turkish pool making its interior possibly the most dramatically beautiful of Budapest's baths. A high, dome roof admits pinpricks of bluish-green light into the dark, circular stone hall with its austere columns and arches. Fed by eight springs with a year-round temperature of 44°C (111°F), the Rudas's highly fluoridated waters have been known for 1,000 years. The facility is open to men only (it does not have a large gay following); a less interesting outer swimming pool is open to both sexes (☞ Outdoor Activities and Sports). Massages are available. I, *Döbrentei tér 9, tel. 1/356–1322. 650 Ft. Weekdays 6 AM–6 PM, weekends 6–noon.*

13 SEMMELWEIS ORVOSTÖRTÉNETI MÚZEUM (Semmelweis Museum of Medical History). This splendid Baroque house was the birthplace of Ignác Semmelweis (1818–1865), the Hungarian physician who proved the contagiousness of puerperal (childbed) fever. It's now a museum that traces the history of healing. Semmelweis's grave is in the garden. *Apród u. 1–3, tel. 1/375–3533. 150 Ft. Tues.–Sun. 10:30–5:30.*

SZABADSÁG SZOBOR (Liberation Monument). Visible from many parts of the city, this 130-ft-high memorial, which starts just below the southern edge of the Citadella, was originally planned as a memorial to a son of Hungary's then-ruler, Miklós Horthy, whose warplane had crashed in the Ukraine in 1942. However, by the time of its completion in 1947 (three years after Horthy was ousted), it had become a memorial to the Russian soldiers who fell in the 1944–45 siege of Budapest; and hence for decades was associated chiefly with this. From afar it looks light, airy, and even liberating. A sturdy young girl, her hair and robe swirling in the wind, holds a palm branch high above her head. Until recently, she was further embellished with sculptures of giants slaying dragons, Red Army soldiers, and peasants rejoicing at the freedom that Soviet liberation promised (but failed) to bring to Hungary. Since 1992, her mood has lightened: In the Budapest city government's systematic purging of

Communist symbols, the Red Combat infantrymen who had flanked the Liberation statue for decades were hacked off and carted away. A few are now on display among the other evicted statues in Szobor Park in the city's 22nd district (☞ Off the Beaten Path, *below*). *Gellért-hegy.*

OFF THE BEATEN PATH **SZOBOR PARK (Statue Park)** – For a look at Budapest's too-recent Iron Curtain past, make the 30-minute drive out to this open-air exhibit, cleverly nicknamed "Tons of Socialism," where 42 of the Communist statues and memorials that once dominated the city's streets and squares have been put out to pasture since the political changes in 1989. Here you can wander among mammoth Lenin and Marx statues and buy socialist-nostalgia souvenirs while songs from the Hungarian and Russian workers' movements play bombastically in the background. *XXII, Balatoni út, corner of Szabadkai út, tel.* 1/227–7446. 250 *Ft. Mar.–mid-Nov., daily* 8–*dusk; mid-Nov.–Feb., weekends* 10–*dusk.*

⓮ **TABÁN PLÉBÁNIA-TEMPLOM** (Tabán Parish Church). In 1736, this church was built on the site of a Turkish mosque and subsequently renovated and reconstructed several times. Its present form—mustard-color stone with a rotund, green clock tower—could be described as restrained Baroque. *I, Attila u.* 1.

NORTH BUDA

Most of these sights are along Fő utca (Main Street), a long, straight thoroughfare that starts at the Chain Bridge and runs parallel to the Danube. It is lined on both sides with multistory late-18th-century houses—many darkened by soot and showing their age more than those you've seen in sparklingly restored areas such as Castle Hill. This northbound exploration can be done with the help of Bus 86, which covers the waterfront, or on foot, although distances are fairly great.

Numbers in the text correspond to numbers in the margin and on the Exploring Budapest map.

A Good Walk

Beginning at **Batthyány tér** ㉑, with its head-on view of Parliament across the Danube, continue north on Fő utca, passing (or stopping to bathe at) the famous Turkish **Király-fürdő** ㉒. From **Bem József tér** ㉓, one block north, turn left (away from the river) up Fekete Sas utca, crossing busy Margit körút and turning right, one block past, up Mecset utca. This will take you up the hill to **Gül Baba türbéje** ㉔.

TIMING

The tour can fit easily into a few hours, including a good 1½-hour soak at the baths; expect the walk from Bem József tér up the hill to Gül Baba türbéje to take about 25 minutes. Fő utca and Bem József tér can get congested during rush hours (from around 7:30 AM to 8:30 AM and 4:30 PM to 6 PM). Remember that museums are closed Monday and that the Király Baths are open to men and women on different days of the week.

Sights to See

㉑ **BATTHYÁNY TÉR.** This lovely square, open on its riverside, affords a grand view of Parliament, directly across the Danube. The M2 subway, the HÉV electric railway from Szentendre, and various suburban and local buses converge on the square, as do peddlers hawking everything from freshly picked flowers to mismatched pairs of shoes. At No. 7 Batthyány tér is the beautiful, Baroque twin-tower **Szent Anna-templom** (Church of St. Anne), dating from 1740–1762, its oval cupola adorned with frescoes and statuary.

NEED A BREAK? The **Angelika** café (II, Batthyány tér 7, tel. 1/212–3784), housed in the Church of St. Anne building, serves swirled meringues, chestnut-filled layer cakes, and a plethora of other heavenly pastries, all baked on the premises from family recipes. You can sit inside on small velvet chairs at marble-top tables or at one of the umbrella-shaded tables outdoors. It's open daily 10 AM–10 PM.

- -

㉓ BEM JÓZSEF TÉR. This square near the river is not particularly picturesque and can get heavy with traffic, but it houses the statue of its important namesake, Polish general József Bem, who offered his services to the 1848 revolutionaries in Vienna and then Hungary. Reorganizing the rebel forces in Transylvania, he was the war's most successful general. It was at this statue on October 23, 1956, that a great student demonstration in sympathy with the Poles' striving for liberal reforms exploded into the brave and tragic Hungarian uprising suppressed by the Red Army.

⑲ CORVIN TÉR. This small, shady square on Fő utca is the site of the turn-of-the-20th-century Folk Art Association administration building and the Budai Vigadó concert hall (☞ Nightlife and the Arts) at No. 8.

㉔ GÜL BABA TÜRBÉJE (Tomb of Gül Baba). Gül Baba, a 16th-century dervish and poet whose name means "father of roses" in Turkish, was buried in a tomb built of carved stone blocks with four oval windows. He fought in several wars waged by the Turks and fell during the siege of Buda in 1541. The tomb remains a place of pilgrimage; it is considered Europe's northernmost Muslim shrine and marks the spot where he was slain. Set at an elevation on Rózsadomb (Rose Hill), the tomb is near a good lookout for city views. II, *Mecset u. 14, tel.* 1/355–8764. *100 Ft. May–Oct., Tues.–Sun.* 10–4.

☾ GYERMEK VASÚT (Children's Railway). The 12-km (7-mi) Children's Railway runs from Széchenyi-hegy to Hűvösvölgy. The sweeping views make the trip well worthwhile for children and adults alike. Departures are from Széchenyi-hegy; to get there, take a cog railway (public transport tickets valid) uphill to the last stop and walk a few hundred yards down a short, partly forested road to the left, in the direction most others will be going. *Cog* railway station: intersection of Szillágyi Erzsébet fasor and Pasaréti út. Children's Railway: about 140 Ft. one-way. Trains run (from Széchenyi-hegy) late Apr.–Oct., daily 8:45–5; Nov.–mid-Mar., Tues.–Fri. 10–4, weekends 10–5 (sometimes closed Tues.); mid-Mar.–late Apr., Tues.–Fri. 9:30–5, weekends 10–5.

OFF THE
BEATEN
PATH

JÁNOSHEGY (Janos Hill) – A libegő (chairlift) will take you to Janos Hill—at 1,729 ft, the highest point in Budapest—where you can climb a lookout tower for the best view of the city. Chairlift: Zugligeti út 97 (take Bus 158 from Moszkva tér to the last stop, Zugligeti út, tel. 1/394–3764. One-way 250 Ft., round-trip 450 Ft. Mid-May–Aug., daily 9–6; Sept.–mid-May (depending on weather), daily 9:30–4; closed every other Mon.

KAPUCINUS TEMPLOM (Capuchin Church). This church was converted from a Turkish mosque at the end of the 17th century. Damaged during the revolution in 1849, it acquired its current romantic-style exterior when it was rebuilt a few years later. II, Fő u. 32.

㉒ KIRÁLY-FÜRDŐ (King Baths). The royal gem of Turkish baths in Budapest was built in the 16th century by the Turkish pasha of Buda. Its stone cupola, crowned by a golden moon and crescent, arches over the steamy, dark pools indoors. It is open to men on Monday, Wednesday, and Friday; to women on Tuesday, Thursday, and Saturday (☞ Outdoor Activities and Sports). These baths are very popular with the gay community. II, Fő u. 84, tel. 1/202–3688. 500 Ft. Weekdays 6:30 AM–6 PM, Sat. 6:30–noon.

㉑ SZILÁGYI DEZSŐTÉR. This is another of the charming little squares punctuating Fő utca; here you'll find the house where composer Béla Bartók lived, at No. 4.

MARGIT-SZIGET (MARGARET ISLAND)

More than 2½ km (1½ mi) long and covering nearly 200 acres, **Margit-sziget** ㉕ is ideal for strolling, jogging, sunbathing, or just loafing. In good weather, the island draws a multitudinous cross section of the city's population out to its gardens and sporting facilities. The outdoor pool complex of the Palatinus Baths (toward the Buda side), built in 1921, can attract tens of thousands of people on a summer day. Nearby are a tennis stadium, a youth athletic center, boathouses, sports grounds, and, most impressive of all, the Nemzeti Sportuszoda (National Sports Swimming Pool), designed by the architect Alfred Hajós (while still in his teens, Hajós won two gold medals in swimming at the first modern Olympic Games, held in Athens in 1896). In addition, walkers, joggers, bicyclists, and rollerbladers do laps around the island's perimeter and up and down the main road, closed to traffic except for Bus 26 (and a few official vehicles), which travels up and down the island and across the Margaret Bridge to and from Pest.

The island's natural curative hot springs have given rise to the Danubius Grand and Thermal hotels on the northern end of the island (☞ Where to Stay) and are piped in to two spa hotels on the mainland, the Aquincum on the Buda bank and the Hélia on the Pest side.

A Good Walk

Entering the island from its southern end at the **Margit híd,** stroll (or rent a bicycle and pedal) north along any of the several tree-shaded paths, including the **Művész sétány,** pausing for a picnic on an open lawn, and eventually ending up at the rock garden at the northern end. From here, you can wander back to the southern end or take Bus 26 on the island's only road.

TIMING

A leisurely walk simply from one end to the other would take about 40 minutes, but it's nice to spend extra time wandering.

To experience Margaret Island's role in Budapest life fully, go on a Saturday or Sunday afternoon to join and/or watch people whiling away the day. Sunday is a particularly good choice for strategic sightseers, who can utilize the rest of the week to cover those city sights and areas that are closed on Sunday. On weekdays, you'll share the island only with joggers and children playing hooky from school.

Sights to See

MARGIT HÍD (Margaret Bridge). At the southern end of the island, the Margaret Bridge is the closer of the two entrances for those coming from downtown Buda or Pest. Just north of the Chain Bridge, the bridge walkway provides gorgeous midriver views of Castle Hill and Parliament. Toward the end of 1944, the bridge was blown up by the retreating Nazis while it was crowded with rush-hour traffic. It was rebuilt in the same unusual shape—forming an obtuse angle in midstream, with a short leg leading down to the island. The original bridge was built during the 1840s by French engineer Ernest Gouin in collaboration with Gustave Eiffel.

25 MARGIT-SZIGET (Margaret Island). The island was first mentioned almost 2,000 years ago as the summer residence of the commander of the Roman garrison at nearby Aquincum. Later known as Rabbit Island (Insula Leporum), it was a royal hunting ground during the Árpád dynasty. King Imre, who reigned from 1196 to 1204, held court here, and several convents and monasteries were built here during the Middle Ages. (During a walk round the island, you'll see the ruins of a few of these buildings.) It takes its current name from St. Margaret, the pious daughter of King Béla IV, who at the ripe old age of 10 retired to a Dominican nunnery here.

MAROSVÁSÁRHELYI ZENÉLŐ KÚT (Marosvásárhely Musical Fountain). At the northern end of the island is a copy of the water-powered Marosvásárhely Musical Fountain, which plays songs and chimes. The original was designed more than 150 years ago by a Transylvanian named Péter Bodor. It stands near a serene, artificial **rock garden** with Japanese dwarf trees and lily ponds. The stream coursing through it never freezes, for it comes from a natural hot spring causing it instead to give off thick steam in winter that enshrouds the garden in a mystical cloud.

MŰVÉSZ SÉTÁNY (Artists' Promenade). Through the center of the island runs the Artists' Promenade, lined with busts of Hungarian visual artists, writers, and musicians. Shaded by giant plane trees, it's a perfect place to stroll. The promenade passes close to the **rose garden** (in the center of the island), a large grassy lawn surrounded by blooming flower beds planted with hundreds of kinds of flowers. It's a great spot to picnic or to watch a game of soccer or Ultimate Frisbee, both of which are regularly played here on weekend afternoons.

DOWNTOWN PEST AND THE KIS KÖRÚT (LITTLE RING ROAD)

Budapest's urban heart is full of bona fide sights plus innumerable tiny streets and grand avenues where you can wander for hours admiring the city's stately old buildings— some freshly sparkling after their first painting in decades, others silently but still gracefully crumbling.

Dominated by the Parliament building, the district surrounding Kossuth tér is the legislative, diplomatic, and administrative nexus of Budapest; most of the ministries are here, as are the National Bank and Courts of Justice. Downriver, the romantic Danube promenade, the Duna korzó, extends along the stretch of riverfront across from Castle Hill. With Vörösmarty tér and pedestrian shopping street Váci utca just inland, this area forms Pest's tourist core. Going south, the korzó ends at Március 15 tér. One block in from the river, Ferenciek tere marks the beginning of the university area, spreading south of Kossuth Lajos utca. Here, the streets are narrower and the sounds of your footsteps echo off the elegantly aging stone buildings.

Pest is laid out in broad circular körúts ("ring roads" or boulevards). Vámház körút is the first sector of the 2½-km (1½-mi) Kis körút (Little Ring Road), which traces the route of the Old Town wall from Szabadság híd (Liberty Bridge) to Deák tér. Construction of the inner körút began in 1872 and was completed in 1880. Changing names as it curves, after Kálvin tér it becomes Múzeum körút (passing by the National Museum), and then Károly körút for its final stretch ending at Deák tér. Deák tér, the only place where all three subway lines converge, could be called the dead-center of downtown. East of Károly körút are the weathered streets of Budapest's former ghetto.

A Good Walk

Starting at Kossuth tér to see the **Országház** ㉖ and the **Néprajzi Múzeum** ㉗, it's worth walking a few blocks southeast to take in stately **Szabadság tér** ㉘ before heading back to the Danube and south to the foot of the **Széchenyi Lánchíd** at **Roosevelt tér** ㉙. As this tour involves quite a bit of walking, you may want to take Tram 2 from Kossuth tér a few stops downriver to Roosevelt tér to save your energy. While time and/or energy may not allow it just now, at some point during your visit, a walk across the Chain Bridge is a must. From Roosevelt tér go south, across the street, and join the **korzó** ㉚ along the river, strolling past the **Vigadó** ㉛ at Vigadó tér, all the way to the **Belvárosi plébánia templom** ㉜ at Március 15 tér, just under the Elizabeth Bridge. Double back up the korzó to Vigadó tér and walk in from the river on Vigadó utca to **Vörösmarty tér** ㉝.

Follow the crowds down pedestrian-only **Váci utca** ㉞, crossing busy Kossuth Lajos utca near Ferenciek tere and continuing along Váci utca's southern stretch to the **Vásárcsarnok** ㊱. Doubling back a few blocks on Váci utca, turn right onto Szerb utca and stroll past the **Szerb Ortodox templom** to the street's end at **Egyetem tér** ㊲. Here, you are going through the darker, narrower streets of this student-filled, increasingly trendy area. A detour into any of the other side streets will give you a good flavor of the area. Walking south on Kecskeméti utca, you will reach **Kálvin tér** ㊳. To save time and energy, you can also take Tram 47 or 49 from Fővám tér, in front of the Vásárcsarnok, one stop away from the Danube to Kálvin tér. Just north of Kálvin tér on Múzeum körút is the **Magyar Nemzeti Múzeum** ㊴. The **Nagy Zsinagóga** ㊵ is about ¾ km (⅓ mi) farther north along the Kis körút (Little Ring Road)—a longish walk or one short stop by tram. From here, more walking along the körút, or a tram ride to the last stop, brings you to Pest's main hub, Deák tér. The **Szent István Bazilika** ㊸ is an extra but rewarding 500-yard walk north on Bajcsy-Zsilinszky út.

TIMING
This is a particularly rich part of the city; the suggested walk will take the better part of a day, including time to visit the museums, stroll on the korzó, and browse on Vaci utca—not to mention time for lunch. Keep in mind that the museums are closed on Monday.

Sights to See

㉜ **BELVÁROSI PLÉBÁNIA TEMPLOM** (Inner City Parish Church). Dating to the 12th century, this is the oldest ecclesiastical building in Pest. It's actually built on something even older—the remains of the Contra Aquincum, a 3rd-century Roman fortress and tower, parts of which are visible next to the church. There is hardly any architectural style that cannot be found in some part or another, starting with a single Romanesque arch in its south tower. The single nave still has its original Gothic chancel and some 15th-century Gothic frescoes. Two side chapels contain beautifully carved Renaissance altarpieces and tabernacles of red marble from the early 16th century. During Budapest's years of Turkish occupation, the church served as a mosque—a *mihrab*, a Muslim prayer niche, is a reminder of this. During the 18th century, the church was given two Baroque towers and its present facade. In 1808 it was enriched with a rococo pulpit, and still later a superb winged triptych was added to the main altar. From 1867 to 1875,

Franz Liszt lived only a few steps away from the church, in a town house where he held regular "musical Sundays" at which Richard and Cosima Wagner were frequent guests and participants. Liszt's own musical Sunday mornings often began in this church. An admirer of its acoustics and organ, he conducted many masses here, including the first Budapest performance of his *Missa Choralis*, in 1872. V, *Március 15 tér 2, tel. 1/318–3108.*

37 **EGYETEM TÉR** (University Square). Budapest's University of Law sits here in the heart of the city's university neighborhood. On one corner is the cool gray-and-green marble **Egyetemi Templom** (University Church), one of Hungary's most beautiful Baroque buildings. Built between 1725 and 1742, it has an especially splendid pulpit.

42 **EVANGÉLIKUS TEMPLOM AND EVANGÉLIKUS MÚZEUM** (Lutheran Church and Lutheran Museum). The neoclassical Lutheran Church sits in the center of it all on busy Deák tér. Classical concerts are regularly held here. The church's interior designer, János Krausz, flouted then-traditional church architecture by placing a single large interior beneath the huge vaulted roof structure. The adjoining school is now the Lutheran Museum, which traces the role of Protestantism in Hungarian history and contains Martin Luther's original will. V, *Deák Ferenc tér 4, tel. 1/317–4173. Museum 300 Ft. (includes tour of church). Museum: Mar.–Dec., Tues.–Sun. 10–6; Jan.–Feb. until 5. Church: open only in conjunction with museum visit and during services (Sun. 9, 11, and 6).*

35 **FERENCIEK TEMPLOM** (Franciscan church). This pale-yellow church was built in 1743. On the wall facing Kossuth Lajos utca is a bronze relief showing a scene from the devastating flood of 1838; the detail is so vivid that it almost makes you seasick. A faded arrow below the relief indicates the high-water mark of almost 4 ft. Next to it is the **Nereids Fountain,** a popular meeting place for students from the nearby Eötvös Loránd University. V, *Ferenciek tere.*

NEED A BREAK? Budapest's newest, most touted café, the **Centrál** (V, Károlyi Mihály u. 9, tel. 1/266–4572), is really nothing new: From 1887, famous writers scribbled away here every day. This, not to mention libraries-worth of thoughtful conversation, kept up until the Communists, who disapproved of such gathering places, shut it down in 1949. At the turn of the new millennium it reopened (after a stint as a video arcade) with a bang. Elegant, smoky, and crowded, the Centrál offers time-honored sweets and both traditional and lighter meals.

GÖRÖG ORTODOX TEMPLOM (Greek Orthodox Church). Built at the end of the 18th century in late-Baroque style, the Greek Orthodox Church was remodeled a century later by Miklós Ybl, who designed the Opera House and many other important Budapest landmarks. The church retains some fine wood carvings and a dazzling array of icons by a late-18th-century Serbian master Miklós Jankovich. V, *Petőfi tér 2/b.*

③⑧ **KÁLVIN TÉR** (Calvin Square). Calvin Square takes its name from the neoclassical Protestant church that tries to dominate this busy traffic hub; more glaringly noticeable, however, is a Pepsi billboard as tall and wide as the bottom half of the church. The Kecskeméti Kapu, a main gate of Pest, once stood here, as well as a cattle market that was a notorious den of thieves. At the beginning of the 19th century, this was where Pest ended and the prairie began.

★ **③⓪** **KORZÓ** (Promenade). The neighborhood to the south of Roosevelt tér has regained much of its past elegance—if not its architectural grandeur—with the erection of the Atrium Hyatt, Inter-Continental, and Budapest Marriott luxury hotels. Traversing all three and continuing well beyond them is the riverside korzó, a pedestrian promenade lined with park benches and appealing outdoor cafés from which one can enjoy postcard-perfect views of Gellért Hill and Castle Hill directly across the Danube. Try to

Had Dinner Here

take a stroll in the evening, when the views are lit up in shimmering gold. From Eötvös tér to Március 15 ter.

KÖZGAZDAGSÁGI EGYETEM (University of Economics). Just below the Liberty Bridge on the waterfront, the monumental neo-Renaissance building was once the Customs House. Built in 1871–1874 by Miklós Ybl, it is now also known as *közgáz* ("econ."), following a stint during the Communist era as Karl Marx University. V, *Fővám tér*.

MAGYAR NEMZETI MÚZEUM (Hungarian National Museum). Built between 1837 and 1847, the museum is a fine example of 19th-century classicism—simple, well proportioned, and surrounded by a large garden. In front of this building on March 15, 1848, Sándor Petőfi recited his revolutionary poem, the "National Song" ("Nemzeti dal"), and the "12 Points," a list of political demands by young Hungarians calling on the people to rise up against the Hapsburgs. Celebrations of the national holiday commemorating the failed revolution are held on these steps every year on March 15.

What used to be the museum's biggest attraction, the **Szent Korona** (Holy Crown), was moved to the Parliament building in early 2000 to mark the millenary of the coronation of Hungary's first king, St. Stephen (☞ Országház, *below*). The museum still has worthwhile rarities, however, including a completely furnished Turkish tent; masterworks of cabinetmaking and woodcarving, including pews from churches in Nyírbátor and Transylvania; a piano that belonged to both Beethoven and Liszt; and, in the treasury, masterpieces of goldsmithing, among them the 11th-century Constantions Monomachos crown from Byzantium and the richly pictorial 16th-century chalice of Miklós Pálffy. Looking at it is like reading the "Prince Valiant" comic strip in gold. The epic Hungarian history exhibit chronicles, among other things, the end of Communism and the much-celebrated exodus of the Russian troops. IX, *Múzeum krt*.

14–16, tel. 1/327–7773. 400 Ft. Mid-Mar.–mid-Oct., Tues.–Sun. 10–6; mid-Oct.–mid-Mar., Tues.–Sun. 10–5.

★ ㊵ **NAGY ZSINAGÓGA** (Great Synagogue). Seating 3,000, Europe's largest synagogue was designed by Ludwig Förs and built between 1844 and 1859 in a Byzantine-Moorish style described as "consciously archaic Romantic-Eastern." Desecrated by German and Hungarian Nazis, it was painstakingly reconstructed with donations from all over the world; its doors reopened in fall 1996. While it is used for regular services during much of the year, it is generally not used in midwinter as the space is too large to heat; between December and February, visiting hours are erratic. In the courtyard behind the synagogue, a weeping willow made of metal honors the victims of the Holocaust. Liszt and Saint-Saëns are among the great musicians who have played the synagogue's grand organ. VII, Dohány u. 2–8, tel. 1/342–1335. Free. Weekdays 10–3, Sun. 10–3. Closed Jewish holidays and Dec.

★ ㉗ **NÉPRAJZI MÚZEUM** (Museum of Ethnography). The 1890s neoclassical temple formerly housed the Supreme Court. Now an impressive permanent exhibition, "The Folk Culture of the Hungarian People," explains all aspects of peasant life from the end of the 18th century until World War I; explanatory texts are provided in both English and Hungarian. Besides embroideries, pottery, and carvings—the authentic pieces you can't see at touristy folk shops—there are farming tools, furniture, and traditional costumes. The central room of the building alone is worth the entrance fee: a majestic hall with ornate marble staircases and pillars, and towering stained-glass windows. V, Kossuth tér 12, tel. 1/332–6340. 300 Ft. Mar.–mid-Oct., Tues.–Sun. 10–5:30; mid-Oct.–Feb., Tues.–Sun. 10–4:30. Hrs may vary during special exhibits. www.hem.hu/e

★ ㉖ **ORSZÁGHÁZ** (Parliament). The most visible symbol of Budapest's left bank is the huge neo-Gothic Parliament. Mirrored in the Danube much the way Britain's Parliament is reflected by the

Thames, it lies midway between the Margaret and Chain bridges and can be reached by the M2 subway (Kossuth tér station) and waterfront Tram 2. A fine example of historicizing, eclectic fin-de-siècle architecture, it was designed by the Hungarian architect Ímre Steindl and built by a thousand workers between 1885 and 1902. The grace and dignity of its long facade and 24 slender towers, with spacious arcades and high windows balancing its vast central dome, lend this living landmark a refreshingly Baroque spatial effect. The exterior is lined with 90 statues of great figures in Hungarian history; the corbels are ornamented by 242 allegorical statues. Inside are 691 rooms, 10 courtyards, and 29 staircases; some 88 pounds of gold were used for the staircases and halls. These halls are also a gallery of late-19th-century Hungarian art, with frescoes and canvases depicting Hungarian history, starting with Mihály Munkácsy's large painting of the Magyar Conquest of 896.

Since early 2000, Parliament's most sacred treasure has not been the Hungarian legislature but the newly exhibited **Szent Korona** (Holy Crown), which reposes with other royal relics under the cupola. The crown sits like a golden soufflé above a Byzantine band of holy scenes in enamel and pearls and other gems. It seems to date from the 12th century, so it could not be the crown that Pope Sylvester II presented to St. Stephen in the year 1000, when he was crowned the first king of Hungary. Nevertheless, it is known as the Crown of St. Stephen and has been regarded—even by Communist governments—as the legal symbol of Hungarian sovereignty and unbroken statehood. In 1945 the fleeing Hungarian army handed over the crown and its accompanying regalia to the Americans rather than have them fall into Soviet hands. They were restored to Hungary in 1978. Through at least August 20, 2001 the crown can be seen in the scope of daily tours of the Parliament building, except during ceremonial events and when the legislature is in session (usually Monday and Tuesday from late summer to spring); its permanent home beyond that date has yet to be decided. Lines may be long, so it's best to call in advance. The building can also be visited on group tours organized by IBUSZ Travel (☞ Visitor Information, in Practical Information). V, Kossuth tér, tel. 1/441–4904 or 1/441–4415. 1,100 Ft.. Daily tours in English at 10 and 2, starting from Gate No. 10, just right of the main stairs. www.mkogy.hu

㉙ ROOSEVELT TÉR (Roosevelt Square). This square opening onto the Danube is less closely connected with the U.S. president than with the progressive Hungarian statesman Count István Széchenyi, dubbed "the greatest Hungarian" even by his adversary, Kossuth. The neo-Renaissance palace of the **Magyar Tudományos Akadémia** (Academy of Sciences) on the north side was built between 1862 and 1864, after Széchenyi's suicide. It is a fitting memorial, for in 1825, the statesman donated a year's income from all his estates to establish the academy. Another Széchenyi project, the Széchenyi Lánchíd (☞ below), leads into the square; there stands a statue of Széchenyi near one of another statesman, Ferenc Deák, whose negotiations led to the establishment of the dual monarchy after Kossuth's 1848–1849 revolution failed. Both men lived on this square.

★ **㉘ SZABADSÁG TÉR** (Liberty Square). This sprawling square is dominated by the longtime headquarters of **Magyar Televízió** (Hungarian Television), a former stock exchange with what look like four temples and two castles on its roof. (At press time the building was due to be auctioned off as the broadcasters move elsewhere.) Across from it is a solemn-looking neoclassical shrine, the **Nemzeti Bank** (National Bank). The bank's Postal Savings Bank branch, adjacent to the main building but visible from behind Szabadság tér on Hold utca, is another exuberant Art Nouveau masterpiece of architect Ödön Lechner, built in 1901 with colorful majolica mosaics, characteristically curvaceous windows, and pointed towers ending in swirling gold flourishes. In the square's center remains one of the few monuments to the Russian "liberation" that were spared the cleansing of symbols of one-party rule. The decision to retain this obelisk—primarily because it marks a gravesite of fallen Soviet troops—caused outrage among some groups. With the Stars and Stripes flying out in front, the **American Embassy** is at Szabadság tér 12.

SZÉCHENYI LÁNCHÍD (Chain Bridge). This is the oldest and most beautiful of the seven road bridges that span the Danube in Budapest. Before it was built, the river could be crossed only by ferry or by a pontoon bridge that had to be removed when ice blocks began floating downstream in winter. It was constructed at the initiative of the great Hungarian reformer and philanthropist Count István Széchenyi, using an 1839 design by the French civil engineer William Tierney Clark. This classical, almost poetically graceful and symmetrical suspension bridge was finished by his Scottish namesake, Adam Clark, who also built the 383-yard tunnel under Castle Hill, thus connecting the Danube quay with the rest of Buda. After it was destroyed by the Nazis, the bridge was rebuilt in its original form (though slightly widened for traffic) and was reopened in 1949, on the centenary of its inauguration. At the Buda end of the bridge is **Clark Ádám tér** (Adam Clark Square), where you can zip up to Castle Hill on the sometimes crowded Sikló funicular. *250 Ft. Funicular daily 7:30 AM–10 PM; closed every other Mon.*

43 **SZENT ISTVÁN BAZILIKA** (St. Stephen's Basilica). Handsome and massive, this is one of the chief landmarks of Pest and the city's largest church—it can hold 8,500 people. Its very Holy Roman front porch greets you with a tympanum bustling with statuary. The basilica's dome and the dome of Parliament are by far the most visible in the Pest skyline, and this is no accident: With the Magyar Millennium of 1896 in mind (the lavishly celebrated thousandth anniversary of the settling of the Carpathian Basin in 896), both domes were planned to be 315 ft high.

The millennium was not yet in sight when architect József Hild began building the basilica in neoclassical style in 1851, two years after the revolution was suppressed. After Hild's death, the project was taken over in 1867 by Miklós Ybl, the architect who did the most to transform modern Pest into a monumental metropolis. Wherever he could, Ybl shifted Hild's motifs toward the neo-Renaissance mode that Ybl favored. When the dome collapsed, partly damaging the walls, he made even more drastic changes. Ybl died in 1891, five years before the 1,000-year celebration, and the basilica was completed in neo-Renaissance style by József Kauser—but not until 1905.

Below the cupola is a rich collection of late-19th-century Hungarian art: mosaics, altarpieces, and statuary (what heady days the Magyar Millennium must have meant for local talents!). There are 150 kinds of marble, all from Hungary except for the Carrara in the sanctuary's centerpiece: a white statue of King (St.) Stephen I, Hungary's first king and patron saint. Stephen's mummified right hand is preserved as a relic in the **Szent Jobb Kápolna** (Holy Right Chapel); press a button and it will be illuminated for two minutes. Visitors can also climb the 364 stairs (or take the elevator) to the top of the cupola for a spectacular view of the city. Extensive restorations have been under way at the aging basilica for years and should wrap up within this decade. *V, Szt. István tér, tel. 1/311–0839. Church free, Szt. Jobb chapel 100 Ft., cupola 400 Ft. Church Mon.–Sat. 9–7, Sun. 1–5; Szt. Jobb Chapel Apr.–Sept., Mon.–Sat. 9–5, Sun. 1–5; Oct.–Mar., Mon.–Sat. 10–4, Sun. 1–4; Cupola Apr. and Sept.–Oct., daily 10–5; May–Aug., daily 9–6.*

SZERB ORTODOX TEMPLOM (Serbian Orthodox Church). Built in 1688, this lovely burnt-orange church, one of Budapest's oldest buildings, sits in a shaded garden surrounded by thick stone walls of the same color detailed with large-tile mosaics and wrought-iron gates. *V, Szerb u.*

34 VÁCI UTCA. Immediately north of Elizabeth Bridge is Budapest's best-known shopping street and most unabashed tourist zone, Váci utca, a pedestrian precinct with electrified 19th-century lampposts and smart shops with credit-card emblems on ornate doorways. No bargain basement, Váci utca gets its special flavor from the mix of native furriers, tailors, designers, shoemakers, and folk artists, as well as an increasing number of internationally known boutiques. There are also bookstores and china and crystal shops, as well as gourmet food stores redolent of paprika. Váci utca's second half, south of Kossuth Lajos utca, was transformed into another pedestrian-only zone a few years ago: This somewhat broader stretch of road, while coming to resemble the northern side, still retains a flavorful, more soothing ambiance of its own. On both halves of Váci utca, watch your purses and wallets—against inflated prices *and* active pickpockets. *V, from Vörösmarty tér to Fővám tér.*

㊶ VÁROSHÁZ (City Hall). The monumental former city council building, which used to be a hospital for wounded soldiers and then a resort for the elderly ("home" would be too cozy for so vast a hulk), is now Budapest's city hall. It's enormous enough to loom over the row of shops and businesses lining Károly körút in front of it but can only be entered through courtyards or side streets (it is most accessible from Gerlóczy utca). The Tuscan columns at the main entrance and the allegorical statuary of *Atlas, War,* and *Peace* are especially splendid. There was once a chapel in the center of the main facade, but now only its spire remains. *V, Városház u. 9–11, tel. 1/327–1000.*

㊱ VÁSÁRCSARNOK (Central Market Hall). The magnificent hall, a 19th-century iron-frame construction, was reopened in late 1994 after years of renovation (and disputes over who would foot the bill). Even during the leanest years of Communist shortages, the abundance of food came as a revelation to shoppers from East and West. Today, the cavernous, three-story market once again teems with people browsing among stalls packed with salamis and red-paprika chains. Upstairs you can buy folk embroideries and souvenirs. *IX, Vámház krt. 1–3. Mon. 6–5, Tues.–Fri. 6 AM–6 PM, Sat. 6–2.*

③ **VIGADÓ** (Concert Hall). Designed in a striking romantic style by Frigyes Feszl and inaugurated in 1865 with Franz Liszt conducting his own *St. Elizabeth Oratorio*, the concert hall is a curious mixture of Byzantine, Moorish, Romanesque, and Hungarian motifs, punctuated by dancing statues and sturdy pillars. Brahms, Debussy, and Casals are among the other phenomenal musicians who have graced its stage. Mahler's *Symphony No. 1* and many works by Bartók were first performed here. While you can go into the lobby on your own, the hall is open only for concerts. V, *Vigadó tér 2.*

★ ③ **VÖRÖSMARTY TÉR** (Vörösmarty Square). This large, handsome square at the northern end of Váci utca is the heart of Pest's tourist life. Street musicians and sidewalk cafés make it one of the liveliest places in Budapest and a good spot to sit and relax—if you can ward off the aggressive caricature sketchers. Grouped around a white-marble statue of the 19th-century poet and dramatist Mihály Vörösmarty are luxury shops, an airline office, and an elegant former pissoir. Now a lovely kiosk, it displays gold-painted historic scenes of the square's golden days. V, *at northern end of Váci u.*

. . . .

NEED A BREAK? The best-known, tastiest, and most tasteful address on Vörösmarty Square belongs to the **Gerbeaud** pastry shop (V, Vörösmarty tér 7, tel. 1/429–9000), founded in 1858 by a French confectioner and later taken over by the Swiss family Gerbeaud. Filling most of a square block, it offers dozens of sweets (as well as sandwiches, coffee, and other not so sugary snacks), served in a salon with green-marble tables and Regency-style marble fireplaces or at tables outside in summer. A mildly hostile staff is an integral part of the Gerbeaud tradition.

. . . .

ZSIDÓ MÚZEUM (Jewish Museum). The four-room museum, around the corner from the Great Synagogue (☞ *above*) has displays explaining the effect of the Holocaust on Hungarian and Transylvanian Jews. (There are labels in English.) In late 1993, burglars ransacked the museum and got away with approximately 80% of its priceless collection; several months later, the stolen objects were found in Romania and returned to their home. Dohány u. 2, tel. 1/342–8949. 600 Ft. Mid-Mar.–mid-Oct., Mon.–Thurs. 10–5, Fri. and Sun. 10–3; mid-Oct.–mid-Mar., weekdays 10–3, Sun. 10–1.

ANDRÁSSY ÚT

Behind St. Stephen's Basilica, at the crossroad along Bajcsy-Zsilinszky út, begins Budapest's grandest avenue, **Andrássy út**. For too many years, this broad boulevard bore the tongue-twisting name of Népköztársaság útja (Avenue of the People's Republic) and, for a while before that, Stalin Avenue. In 1990, however, it reverted to its old name honoring Count Gyula Andrássy, a statesman who in 1867 became the first constitutional premier of Hungary. The boulevard that would eventually bear his name was begun in 1872, as Buda and Pest (and Óbuda) were about to be unified. Most of the mansions that line it were completed by 1884. It took another dozen years before the first **underground railway** on the Continent was completed for—you guessed it—the Magyar Millennium in 1896. Though preceded by London's Underground (1863), Budapest's was the world's first electrified subway. Only slightly modernized but refurbished for the 1996 millecentenary, this "Little Metro" is still running a 4-km (2½-mi) stretch from Vörösmarty tér to the far end of City Park. Using tiny yellow trains with tanklike treads, and stopping at antique stations marked FÖLDALATTI (Underground) on their wrought-iron entranceways, Line 1 is a tourist attraction in itself. Six of its 10 stations are along Andrássy út.

A Good Walk

A walking tour of Andrássy út's sights is straightforward: Begin at its downtown end, near Deák tér, and stroll its length (about 2 km/1¼ mi) all the way to Hősök tere. The first third of the avenue, from Bajcsy-Zsilinszky út to the eight-sided intersection called Oktogon, boasts a row of eclectic city palaces with balconies held up by stone giants. Pause at the **Magyar Állami Operaház** ⑷ and other points along the way. One block past the Operaház, Andrássy út intersects Budapest's Broadway: Nagymező utca contains several theaters, cabarets, and nightclubs. Andrássy út alters when it crosses the Nagy körút (Outer Ring Road), at the Oktogon crossing. Four rows of trees and scores of flower beds make the thoroughfare look more like a garden promenade, but its cultural character lingers. Farther up, past **Kodály körönd,** the rest of Andrássy út is dominated by widely spaced mansions surrounded by private gardens. At **Hősök tere** ⑷, browse through the **Műcsarnok** ⑷ and/or the **Szépművészeti Múzeum** ⑸, and finish off with a stroll into the Városliget (City Park; ☞ *below*). You can return to Deák tér on the subway, the Millenniumi Földalatti (Millennial Underground).

TIMING

As most museums are closed Monday, it's best to explore Andrássy út on other days, preferably weekdays or early Saturday, when stores are also open for browsing. During opera season, you can time your exploration to land you at the Operaház stairs just before 7 PM to watch the spectacle of operagoers flowing in for the evening's performance.

Sights to See

🕙 **BUDAPEST BÁBSZÍNHÁZ** (Budapest Puppet Theater). In this templelike, eclectic building, you'll find colorful shows that both children and adults enjoy even if they don't understand Hungarian. Watch for showings of *Cinderella* (*Hamupipőke*) and *Snow White and the Seven Dwarfs* (*Hófehérke*), part of the theater's regular repertoire. VI, Andrássy út 69, tel. 1/321–5200.

DRECHSLER KASTÉLY (Drechsler Palace). Across the street from the Operaház is the French Renaissance–style Drechsler Palace. An early work by Ödön Lechner, Hungary's master of Art

Nouveau, it is now the home of the National Ballet School and is generally not open to tourists. VI, *Andrássy út 25*.

HŐSÖK TERE (Heroes' Square). Andrássy út ends in grandeur at Heroes' Square, with Budapest's answer to Berlin's Brandenburg Gate. Cleaned and refurbished in 1996 for the millecentenary, the **Millenniumi Emlékmű** (Millennial Monument) is a semicircular twin colonnade with statues of Hungary's kings and leaders between its pillars. Set back in its open center, a 118-ft stone column is crowned by a dynamic statue of the archangel Gabriel, his outstretched arms bearing the ancient emblems of Hungary. At its base ride seven bronze horsemen: the Magyar chieftains, led by Árpád, whose tribes conquered the land in 896. Before the column lies a simple marble slab, the **Nemzeti Háborús Emlék Tábla** (National War Memorial), the nation's altar, at which every visiting foreign dignitary lays a ceremonial wreath. England's Queen Elizabeth upheld the tradition during her royal visit in May of 1992. In 1991 Pope John Paul II conducted a mass here. Just a few months earlier, half a million Hungarians had convened to recall the memory of Imre Nagy, the reform-minded Communist prime minister who partially inspired the 1956 revolution. Little would anyone have guessed then that in 1995, palm trees, and Madonna, would spring up on this very square in a scene from the film *Evita* (set in Argentina, not Hungary); nor that Michael Jackson would do his part to consecrate the square with a music video. Heroes' Square is flanked by the **Műcsarnok** and the **Szépművészeti Múzeum** (☞ *below*).

KODÁLY KÖRÖND. A handsome traffic circle with imposing statues of three Hungarian warriors—leavened by a fourth one of a poet—Kodály körönd is surrounded by plane and chestnut trees. Look carefully at the towered mansions on the north side of the circle—behind the soot you'll see the fading colors of ornate frescoes peeking through. The circle takes its name from the composer Zoltán Kodály, who lived just beyond it at Andrássy út 89. VI, *Andrássy út at Szinyei Merse u.*.

47 LISZT FERENC EMLÉKMÚZEUM (Franz Liszt Memorial Museum). Andrássy út No. 67 was the original location of the old Academy of Music and Franz Liszt's last home; entered around the corner, it now houses a museum. Several rooms display the original furniture and instruments from Liszt's time there; another room shows temporary exhibits. The museum hosts excellent, free classical concerts year-round, except in August. VI, *Vörösmarty u. 35, tel. 1/342–7320. 200 Ft. Weekdays 10–6, Sat. 9–5. Classical concerts (free with admission) Sept.–July, Sat. 11 AM. Closed Aug. 1–20.*

46 LISZT FERENC ZENEAKADÉMIA (Franz Liszt Academy of Music). Along with the **Vigadó** (☞ Downtown Pest and the Kis körút [Little Ring Road], *above*), this is one of the city's main concert halls. The academy in fact has two auditoriums: a green-and-gold 1,200-seat main hall and a smaller hall for chamber music and solo recitals. Outside this exuberant Art Nouveau building, a statue of Liszt oversees the square. The academy has been operating as a highly revered teaching institute since 1907; Liszt was its first chairman and the composer Ferenc Erkel its first director. The pianist Ernő (formerly Ernst) Dohnányi and composers Béla Bartók and Zoltán Kodály were teachers here. VI, *Liszt Ferenc tér 8, tel. 1/342–0179.*

★ **44 MAGYAR ÁLLAMI OPERAHÁZ** (Hungarian State Opera House). Miklós Ybl's crowning achievement is the neo-Renaissance Opera House, built between 1875 and 1884. Badly damaged during the siege of 1944–1945, it was restored for its 1984 centenary. Two buxom marble sphinxes guard the driveway; the main entrance is flanked by Alajos Stróbl's "romantic-realist" limestone statues of Liszt and of another 19th-century Hungarian composer, Ferenc Erkel, the father of Hungarian opera (his patriotic opera *Bánk bán* is still performed for national celebrations).

Inside, the spectacle begins even before the performance does. You glide up grand staircases and through wood-paneled corridors and gilt lime-green salons into a glittering jewel box of an auditorium. Its four tiers of boxes are held up by helmeted sphinxes beneath a frescoed ceiling by Károly Lotz. Lower down there are frescoes everywhere, with intertwined motifs of Apollo and Dionysus. In its early years, the Budapest Opera was conducted by Gustav Mahler (from 1888 to 1891) and, after World War II, by Otto Klemperer.

The best way to experience the Opera House's interior is to see a ballet or opera; and while performance quality varies, tickets are relatively cheap and easy to come by, at least by tourist standards. And descending from *La Bohème* into the Földalatti station beneath the Opera House was described by travel writer Stephen Brook in *The Double Eagle* as stepping "out of one period piece and into another." There are no performances in summer, except for the week-long BudaFest international opera and ballet festival in mid-August. You cannot view the interior on your own, but forty-five-minute tours in English are usually conducted daily at 3 PM and 4 PM; buy tickets in the Opera Shop, by the sphinx at the Hajós utca entrance. (Large groups should call in advance.) VI, *Andrássy út 22, tel. 1/331–2550 (ext. 156 for tours). Tours 1,000 Ft.*

㊺ MAGYAR FOTÓGRÁFUSOK HÁZA (MAI MANÓ HÁZ) (Hungarian Photographers' House). This ornate turn-of-the-20th-century building was built as a photography studio, where the wealthy bourgeoisie would come to be photographed by imperial and royal court photographer Manó Mai. Inside, ironwork and frescoes ornament the curving staircase leading up to the recently expanded facility, the largest of Budapest's three photo galleries. V, *Nagymező u. 20, tel. 1/302–4398. 200 Ft. Weekdays 2–6.*

NEED A BREAK? The **Lukács** café (VI, Andrássy út 70, tel. 1/302–8747) shares its entrance with an international bank, but its upstairs salon is steeped in classic café elegance. The room is anchored at one end by an ornate fireplace; you can recharge with an espresso at one of the marble-top tables clustered under a sparkling chandelier. The Lukács was built in 1912, during Budapest's café-culture glory days, but in the repressive 1950s it was taken over by the secret police to serve as a meeting spot. To many locals, it still evokes those dark times.

....

49 MŰCSARNOK (Palace of Exhibitions). The city's largest hall for special exhibitions is a striking 1895 temple of culture with a colorful tympanum. Its program of events includes exhibitions of contemporary Hungarian and international art and a rich series of films, plays, and concerts. *XIV, Hősök tere, tel. 1/343–7401. 300 Ft., free Tues. Tues.–Sun. 10–6.*

50 SZÉPMŰVÉSZETI MÚZEUM (Museum of Fine Arts). Across Heroes' Square from the Palace of Exhibitions and built by the same team of Albert Schickedanz and Fülöp Herzog, the Museum of Fine Arts houses Hungary's finest collection, rich in Flemish and Dutch old masters. With seven fine El Grecos and five beautiful Goyas as well as paintings by Velázquez and Murillo, the collection of Spanish old masters is one of the best outside Spain. The Italian school is represented by Giorgione, Bellini, Correggio, Tintoretto, and Titian masterpieces and, above all, two superb Raphael paintings: *Eszterházy Madonna* and his immortal *Portrait of a Youth*, rescued after a world-famous art heist. Nineteenth-century French art includes works by Delacroix, Pissarro, Cézanne, Toulouse-Lautrec, Gauguin, Renoir, and Monet. There are also more than 100,000 drawings (including five by Rembrandt and three studies by Leonardo), Egyptian and Greco-Roman exhibitions, late-Gothic winged altars from northern Hungary and Transylvania, and works by all the leading figures of Hungarian art up to the present. A 20th-century collection was added to the museum's permanent exhibits in 1994, comprising an interesting series of statues, paintings, and drawings by Chagall, Le Corbusier, and others. Labels are in both Hungarian and English; there's also an English-language booklet for sale about the permanent collection. *XIV, Hősök tere, tel. 1/343–9759. 500 Ft. Tues.–Sun. 10–5:30.*

VÁROSLIGET (CITY PARK) ✓

Heroes' Square is the gateway to the **Városliget** (City Park): a square km (almost ⅓ square mi) of recreation, entertainment, beauty, and culture. A bridge behind the Millennial Monument leads across a boating basin that becomes an artificial ice-skating rink in winter; to the south of this lake stands a statue of George Washington, erected in 1906 with donations by Hungarian emigrants to the United States. Next to the lake stands **Vajdahunyad Vár,** built in myriad architectural styles. Visitors can soak or swim at the turn-of-the-20th-century Széchenyi Fürdő, jog along the park paths, or careen on Vidám Park's roller coaster. There's also the Petőfi Csarnok, a leisure-time youth center and major concert hall on the site of an old industrial exhibition.

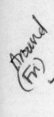

TIMING

Fair-weather weekends, when the children's attractions are teeming with youngsters and parents and the Széchenyi Fürdő brimming with bathers, are the best time for people-watchers to visit City Park; if you go on a weekday, the main sights are rarely crowded.

Sights to See

BUDAPESTI ÁLLATKERT (Budapest Zoo). The renovation that began in this once depressing urban zoo in the late 1990s is expected to take until 2004, but the place is already cheerier, at least for humans—petting opportunities aplenty, and a new monkey-house where endearing, seemingly clawless little simians climb all over you (beware of pickpockets!). Don't miss the elephant pavilion, decorated with Zsolnay majolica and glazed ceramic animals. *XIV, Állatkerti krt. 6–12, tel. 1/343–6075. 650 Ft. Mar. and Oct., daily 9–5; Apr. and Sept., daily 9–6; May, daily 9–6:30; June–Aug., daily 9–7; Nov.–Feb., daily 9–4 (last tickets sold 1 hr before closing).*

FŐVÁROSI NAGYCIRKUSZ (Municipal Grand Circus). Colorful performances by local acrobats, clowns, and animal trainers, as well as by international guests, are staged here in a small ring. XIV, Állatkerti krt. 7, tel. 1/343–9630. *Weekdays 500–900 Ft., weekends 550–950 Ft. July–Aug., Wed.–Fri. 3 and 7, Thu. 3, Sat. 10, 3, and 7, Sun. 10 and 3; Nov.–June, schedule varies.*

SZÉCHENYI FÜRDŐ (Széchenyi Baths). Dating from 1876, these vast baths are in a beautiful neo-Baroque building in the middle of City Park; they comprise one of the biggest spas in Europe. There are several thermal pools indoors as well as two outdoors, which remain open even in winter, when dense steam hangs thick over the hot water's surface—you can just barely make out the figures of elderly men, submerged shoulder deep, crowded around waterproof chessboards (☞ Outdoor Activities and Sports). XIV, Állatkerti krt. 11, tel. 1/321–0310. *400 Ft. (changing room), 700 Ft. (cabin). Weekdays 6 AM–6 PM, weekends 6–5.*

VAJDAHUNYAD VÁR (Vajdahunyad Castle). Beside the City Park's lake stands this castle, an art historian's Disneyland, this fantastic medley borrows from all of Hungary's historic and architectural past, starting with the Romanesque gateway of the cloister of Jak in western Hungary. A Gothic castle, Transylvanian turrets, Renaissance loggia, Baroque portico, and Byzantine decoration are all guarded by a spooky modern (1903) bronze statue of the anonymous medieval chronicler who was the first recorder of Hungarian history. Designed for the millennial celebration in 1896 but not completed until 1908, this hodgepodge houses the surprisingly interesting **Mezőgazdasági Múzeum** (Agricultural Museum), with intriguingly arranged sections on animal husbandry, forestry, horticulture, hunting, and fishing. XIV, Városliget, Széchenyi Island, tel. 1/343–3198. *Museum 200 Ft. Mid-Feb.–mid-Nov., Tues.–Fri. and Sun. 10–5, Sat. 10–6; mid-Nov.–mid-Feb., Tues.–Fri. 10–4, weekends 10–5.*

☾ **VIDÁM PARK.** Budapest's somewhat weary amusement park is next to the zoo and is crawling with happy children with their parents or grandparents in tow. Rides cost around $1 (some are for preschoolers). There are also game rooms and a scenic railway. Next to the main park is a separate, smaller section for toddlers. In winter, only a few rides operate. *XIV, Városliget, Állatkerti krt. 14–16, tel. 1/343–0996. 100 Ft. Apr.–Oct., daily 10–about 8 (varies); Nov.–Mar., daily 10–late afternoon.*

EASTERN PEST AND THE NAGY KÖRÚT (GREAT RING ROAD)

This section covers primarily Kossuth Lajos–Rákóczi út and the Nagykörút (Great Ring Road)—busy, less-touristy urban thoroughfares full of people, cars, shops, and Budapest's unique urban flavor.

Beginning a few blocks from the Elizabeth Bridge, Kossuth Lajos utca is Budapest's busiest shopping street. Try to look above and beyond the store windows to the architecture and activity along Kossuth Lajos utca and its continuation, Rákóczi út, which begins when it crosses the Kis körút (Little Ring Road) at the busy intersection called Astoria. Most of Rákóczi út is lined with hotels, shops, and department stores and it ends at the grandiose Keleti (East) Railway Station, on Baross tér.

Pest's Great Ring Road, the Nagy körút, was laid out at the end of the 19th century in a wide semicircle anchored to the Danube at both ends; an arm of the river was covered over to create this 114-ft-wide thoroughfare. The large apartment buildings on both sides also date from this era. Along with theaters, stores, and cafés, they form a boulevard unique in Europe for its "unified eclecticism," which blends a variety of historic styles into a harmonious whole. Its entire length of almost 4½ km (2¾ mi) from Margaret Bridge to Petőfi Bridge is traversed by Trams 4 and 6, but strolling it in stretches is also a good way to experience the hustle and bustle of downtown Budapest.

Like its smaller counterpart, the Kis Körút (Little Ring Road), the Great Ring Road comprises sectors of various names. Beginning with Ferenc körút at the Petőfi Bridge, it changes to

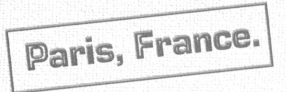

Paris, France.

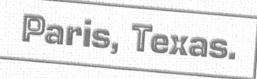

Paris, Texas.

When it Comes to Getting Local Currency at an ATM, Same Thing.

Whether you're in Yosemite or Yemen, using your Visa® card or ATM card with the PLUS symbol is the easiest and most convenient way to get local currency. For example, let's say you're in France. When you make a withdrawal, using your secured PIN, it's dispensed in francs, but is debited from your account in U.S. dollars. This makes it easy to take advantage of favorable exchange rates. And if you need help finding one of Visa's 627,000 ATMs in 127 countries worldwide, visit **visa.com/pd/atm**. We'll make finding an ATM as easy as finding the Eiffel Tower, the Pyramids or even the Grand Canyon.

It's Everywhere You Want To Be.

SEE THE WORLD
IN FULL COLOR

Fodor's Exploring Guides bring all the great sights vividly to life with hundreds of photographs, fascinating historical background, and colorful anecdotes. Detailed maps and practical information keep you headed in the right direction.

Pair a Fodor's Exploring Guide with your trusted Fodor's Pocket Guide for a complete planning package.

Fodor's EXPLORING GUIDES

At bookstores everywhere.

József körút at the intersection marked by the Museum of Applied Arts, then to Erzsébet körút at Blaha Lujza Square. Teréz körút begins at the busy Oktogon crossing with Andrássy út and ends at the Nyugati (West) Railway Station, where Szent Istvan takes over for the final stretch to the Margaret Bridge.

A Good Walk

Beginning with a visit to the **Iparművészeti Múzeum** ㉛, near the southern end of the boulevard, walk or take Tram 4 or 6 north (away from the Petőfi Bridge) to the New York Kávéház on Erzsébet körút, just past Blaha Lujza tér—all in all about 1¾ km (1 mi) from the museum. The neo-Renaissance **Keleti pályaudvar** is a one-metro-stop detour away from Blaha Lujza tér. Continuing in the same direction on the körút, go several stops on the tram to **Nyugati pályaudvar** and walk the remaining sector, Szent István körút, past the **Vígszínház** ㉝ to Margaret Bridge. From the bridge, views of Margaret Island, to the north, and Parliament, Castle Hill, the Chain Bridge, and Gellért Hill, to the south, are gorgeous.

TIMING

As this area is packed with stores, it's best to explore during business hours—weekdays until around 5 PM and Saturday until 1 PM; Saturday will be most crowded. Keep in mind that the Iparművészeti Múzeum is closed Monday.

Sights to See

★ ㉛ **IPARMŰVÉSZETI MÚZEUM** (Museum of Applied and Decorative Arts). The templelike structure housing this museum is indeed a shrine to Hungarian Art Nouveau, and in front of it, drawing pen in hand, sits a statue of its creator, Hungarian architect Ödön Lechner. Opened in the Magyar Millennial year of 1896, it was only the third museum of its kind in Europe. Its dome of tiles is crowned by a majolica lantern from the same source: the Zsolnay ceramic works in Pécs. Inside its central hall are playfully swirling whitewashed, double-decker, Moorish-style galleries and arcades. The museum, which collects and studies objects of interior decoration and use, has five departments: furniture, textiles, goldsmithing, ceramics, and everyday objects. *Üllői út 33–37, tel. 1/217–5222. 300 Ft. Mid-Mar.–Oct., Tues.–Sun. 10–6; Nov.–mid-Mar., Tues.–Sun. 10–4. www.imm.hu*

NEED A BREAK? Once the haunt of famous writers and intellectuals, whose caricatures decorate the walls, now mostly that of tourists—those who manage to find the entrance under the seemingly permanent scaffolding—the **New York Kávéház** (VII, Erzsébet krt. 9–11, tel. 1/322–1648) is an eclectic, neo-Baroque café and restaurant in the ornate 1894 New York Palace building.

KELETI PÁLYAUDVAR (East Railway Station). The grandiose, imperial-looking East Railway Station was built in 1884 and considered Europe's most modern until well into the 20th century. Its neo-Renaissance facade, which resembles a gateway, is flanked by statues of two British inventors and railway pioneers, James Watt and George Stephenson. *VIII, Baross tér.*

52 **KÖZTÁRSASÁG TÉR** (Square of the Republic). Surrounded by faceless concrete buildings, this square is not particularly alluring aesthetically but is significant because it was where the Communist Party of Budapest had its headquarters, and it was also the scene of heavy fighting in 1956. Here also is the city's second opera house, and Budapest's largest, the **Erkel Ferenc színház** (Ferenc Erkel Theater).

NYUGATI PÁLYAUDVAR (West Railway Station). The iron-laced glass hall of the West Railway Station is in complete contrast to—and much more modern than—the newer East Railway Station. Built in the 1870s, it was designed by a team of architects from Gustav Eiffel's office in Paris. *VI, Teréz krt.*

PÁRIZSI UDVAR (Paris Court). This glass-roof arcade was built in 1914 in richly ornamental neo-Gothic and eclectic styles.

Nowadays it's filled with touristy boutiques. *VI, Corner of Petőfi Sándor u. and Kossuth Lajos u.*

. . . .

NEED A BREAK? Hands down the best café in this part of town, the **Európa kávéház** (V, Szent István krt. 7–9, tel. 1/312–2362) has marble-top tables; top-notch elegance; and, yes, delectable sweets. While it seems (in the best sense) a century old, it's in fact only about two years. Here you can sample some Eszterházy torta (a rich, buttery cake with walnut batter and, here at least, a walnut on top) or, say, a Tyrolean strudel with poppy-seed filling.

. . . .

★ ❸ **VÍGSZÍNHÁZ** (Comedy Theater). This neo-Baroque, late-19th-century, gemlike theater twinkles with just a tiny, playful anticipation of Art Nouveau and sparkles inside and out since its 1994 refurbishment. The theater hosts primarily musicals, such as Hungarian adaptations of *Cats*, as well as dance performances and classical concerts. *XIII, Pannónia u. 1, tel. 1/329–2340. www.vigszinhaz.hu*

ÓBUDA

Until its unification with Buda and Pest in 1872 to form the city of Budapest, Óbuda (meaning Old Buda) was a separate town that used to be the main settlement; now it is usually thought of as a suburb. Although the vast new apartment blocks of Budapest's biggest housing project and busy roadways are what first strike the eye, the historic core of Óbuda has been preserved in its entirety.

A Good Walk

Óbuda is easily reached by car, bus, or streetcar via the Árpád Bridge from Pest or by the HÉV suburban railway from Batthyány tér to the Árpád Bridge. Once you're there, covering all the sights on foot involves large but manageable distances along major exhaust-permeated roadways. One way to tackle it is to take Tram 17 from its southern terminus at the Buda side of the Margaret Bridge to Kiscelli utca and walk uphill to the **Kiscelli Múzeum**. Then walk back down the same street all the way past **Flórián tér**, continuing toward the Danube and making a left onto Hídfő utca or Szentlélek tér to enter **Fő tér**. After exploring the square, walk a block or two southeast to the HÉV suburban railway stop and take the train just north to the museum complex at **Aquincum**.

TIMING

It's best to begin touring Óbuda during the cooler, early hours of the day, as the heat on the area's busy roads can get overbearing. Museums are closed on Monday.

Sights to See

AQUINCUM. This complex comprises the reconstructed remains of a Roman settlement dating from the 1st century AD and the capital of the Roman province of Pannonia. Careful excavations have unearthed a varied selection of artifacts and mosaics, giving a tantalizing inkling of what life was like in the provinces of the Roman Empire. A gymnasium and a central heating system have been unearthed, along with the ruins of two baths and a shrine to Mithras, the Persian god of light, truth, and the sun. The **Aquincum múzeum** (Aquincum Museum) displays the dig's most notable finds: ceramics; a red-marble sarcophagus showing a triton and flying Eros on one side and on the other, Telesphorus, the angel of death, depicted as a hooded dwarf; and jewelry from a Roman lady's tomb. III, *Szentendrei út 139, tel. 1/250–1650. 400 Ft. Mid-Apr.–Apr. 30 and Oct., Tues.–Sun. 10–5; May–Sept., Tues.–Sun. 10–6. Grounds open at 9.*

FLÓRIÁN TÉR (Flórián Square). The center of today's Óbuda is Flórián tér, where Roman ruins were first discovered when the foundations of a house were dug in 1778. Two centuries later, careful excavations were carried out during the reconstruction of the square, and today the restored ancient ruins lie in the center of the square in boggling contrast to the racing traffic and cement-block housing projects. III, *Vörösvári út at Pacsirtamező u.*

FŐ TÉR (Main Square). Óbuda's old main square is its most picturesque part. The square has been spruced up in recent years, and there are now several good restaurants and interesting museums in and around the Baroque **Zichy Kúria** (Zichy Mansion), which has become a neighborhood cultural center. Among the most popular offerings are the summer concerts in the courtyard and the evening jazz concerts. III, *Kórház u. at Hídfő u.*

KISCELLI MÚZEUM (Kiscelli Museum). A strenuous climb up the steep, dilapidated sidewalks of Remetehegy (Hermit's Hill) will deposit you at this elegant, mustard-yellow Baroque mansion. Built between 1744 and 1760 as a Trinitarian monastery, today it holds an eclectic mix of paintings, sculptures, engravings, and sundry items related to the history of Budapest. Included here is the printing press on which poet and revolutionary Sándor Petőfi printed his famous "Nemzeti Dal" ("National Song"), in 1848, inciting the Hungarian people to rise up against the Hapsburgs. III, *Kiscelli u. 108, tel. 1/250–0304. 200 Ft. Nov.–Mar., Tues.–Sun. 10–4; Apr.–Oct., Tues.–Sun. 10–6.*

RÓMAI AMFITEÁTRUM (Roman Amphitheater). Probably dating back to the 2nd century, Óbuda's Roman military amphitheater once held some 16,000 people and, at 144 yards in diameter, was one of Europe's largest. A block of dwellings called the Round House was later built by the Romans above the amphitheater; massive stone walls found in the Round House's cellar were actually parts of the amphitheater. Below the amphitheater are the cells where prisoners and lions were held while awaiting confrontation. III, *Pacsirtamező u. at Nagyszombat u.*

In This Chapter

Updated by Betsy Maury

eating out

IN BUDAPEST, numerous new ethnic restaurants—from Chinese to Mexican to Hare Krishna Indian—are springing up all the time. The pulse of the city's increasingly vibrant restaurant scene is in downtown Pest; restaurants on Castle Hill tend to be more touristy and expensive. Our choice of restaurants is primarily Hungarian and Continental, but if you get a craving for sushi or tortellini, consult the restaurant listings in the English-language publications for the latest information on what's cooking where. Remember that some restaurants, particularly the tourist-oriented ones, occasionally fall into the international practice of embellishing tourists' bills. Authorities in Budapest, however, have been cracking down on establishments reported for overcharging. Don't order from menus without prices, and don't accept dining or drinking invitations from anyone hired to lure people into shady situations.

CATEGORY	COST*
$$$$	over $11
$$$	$8–$11
$$	$5–$8
$	under $5

*per person for a three-course meal, excluding wine and tip

DOWNTOWN PEST AND THE LITTLE RING ROAD

$$$–$$$$ MÚZEUM. The gustatory anticipation sparked by this elegant, candlelit salon with mirrors, mosaics, and swift-moving waiters is matched by wholly satisfying, wonderful food. The salads are

Margit-sziget
(Margaret Is.)

Margit híd
(Margaret Br.)

Frankel Leó út.

Rómer Flóris u. (Martírok útja)

Bem József u.

Bem rakpart
Fő u.

Katona József u.

Pannónia u.

Szent István körút

Balaton u.

Szemere u.

Markó u.

Kossuth
Lajos tér

Alkotmány u.

Báthori u.

Zoltán u.

Szabadság
tér

Arany János u.

Nádor u.

PEST

József Attila u.

Erzsébet
tér

Kisrókus u.

Margit körút

Varsányi Irén u. Kacsa u.

Csalogány u.

Moszkva
tér

Batthyány u.

Donáti u.

Szabó Ilonka u.

Táncsics M. u.

Fortuna u.

Úri u.

Országház u.

Tóth Árpád sétány

Lovas

Várhegy

Déli pu.
(South
Station)

Vérmező

Ferenc u.

Hunyadi János út.

BUDA

Fő u.

Dísz
tér

Attila út

Lógodi u.

Clark
Ádám
tér

Széchenyi
lánchíd
(Chain Br.)

Roosevelt

Belgrád

Víziváros

Danube

Széchenyi rakpart

Újpesti rakpart

Alagút u.

Naphegy u.

Krisztina körút

Lisznyai u.

Mészáros u.

Avar u.

Tabán

Gróza P. rakpart

Deák F.

Vörösmarty
tér

Petőfi Sándor u.

Váci utca

Erzsébet híd
(Elizabeth Br.)

Hegyalja út

Tigris u.

Csörsz u.

Öröm u.

Fehér

Molnár u.

TO SZOBOR PARK

KEY

— Rail Lines

ℹ️ Tourist Information

Rippl-Rónai u.

17 **19** Hősök
tere

Városliget

Olof Palme sétány

onia u.

Visegrádi u.

Váci út

Ferdinánd híd

**Nyugati pu.
(West
Station)**

Szinyei Merse u.

Bajza u.

Benczúr u.

Dózsa György út

Ajtósi Dürer sor

Nyugati
tér

Podmaniczky utca

Szondi u.

Rózsa u.

Kodály Körönd

Bajcsy-Zsilinszky út

Teréz körút

Jókai u.

Aradi u.

Andrássy út

Vörösmarty u.

Oktogon

Liszt Ferenc
tér

Erzsébet körút

Kertész u.

Akácfa u.

Felső erdősor

Városligeti fasor

Damjanich u.

Rottenbiller utca

Dembinszky u.

István u.

Dózsa György út

Nagymező u.

Paulay Ede u.

Király u.

Dob utca

Wesselényi utca

Klauzál u.

Dohány utca

Rákóczi út

Thököly út

Verseny u.

**Keleti pu.
(East Station)**

Baross
tér

Kerepesi út

Fiumei út

15 **11**
Deák
tér

Lázár u.

Károly krt.

16

Szentkirályi u.

Puskin u.

József körút

Köztársaság
tér

Népszínház u.

Bérkocsis u.

Kerepesi
temető
(Cemetery)

13
Ferenciek
tere

Petőfi Sándor u.

Kossuth L. u.

Múzeum krt.

14

Bródy Sándor u.

Somogyi Béla u.

Déri Miksa u.

Déri Miksa u.

József u.

Mátyás
tér

Dankó u.

Teleki
László
tér

Lujza u.

Veres Pálné u.

Váci utca

Molnár u.

Kálvin
tér

Krúdy u.

Múzeum u.

Baross utca

Baross utca

0   550 yards

0   500 meters

N

generous, the Hungarian wines excellent, and the chef dares to be creative. VIII, Múzeum krt. 11, tel. 1/267–0375. *Jacket and tie.* AE. *Closed Sun.*

$$$ LOU LOU. ★ This glowing bistro tucked onto a side street near the Danube has been one of the hottest restaurants in Budapest for years. Blending local and Continental cuisines, the menu includes a succulent fresh salmon with lemongrass; the venison fillet with wild berry sauce is another mouthwatering choice. Although recently expanded, Lou Lou retains its intimate charm. V, Vigyázó Ferenc u. 4, tel. 1/312–4505. *Reservations essential.* AE. *No lunch Sat. Closed daily 3–7 and Sun.*

$$$ MŰVÉSZINAS. ★ Walls hung with framed vintage prints and photos, antique vitrines filled with old books, and tall, slender candles on the tables create a romantic haze here. Dozens of Hungarian specialties fill the long menu, from sirloin "Budapest style" (smothered in a goose-liver, mushrooms, and sweet-pepper ragout) to spinach-stuffed turkey breast in garlic sauce. Poppy-seed palacsinta with plum sauce are a sublime dessert. VI, Bajcsy-Zsilinszky út 9, tel. 1/268–1439. *Reservations essential.* AE, MC, V.

$$ AMSTEL RIVER CAFÉ. Just steps from the tourist-filled Vái utca, you'll find this welcoming, low-key Dutch café. The menu has something for everyone—from rabbit to Caesar salad to grilled chicken, served on tables outside in the summer. Besides the Amstel beers (of course), there's a weekly changing wine list. A guitarist serenades with Spanish music on Sundays. V, Párizsi u. 6, tel. 1/266–4334. *No credit cards.*

$$ CAFÉ KÖR. ★ The wrought-iron tables, vault ceilings, and crisp white tablecloths give this chic bistro a decidedly downtown feel. In the heart of the busy fifth district, Café Kör is ideal for lunch or dinner when touring nearby Andrássy út or St. Stephen's Basilica. The Café Kör specialty plate is a feast of rich goose liver paté, grilled meats, and cheeses, to be savored with a glass of Hungarian *pezsgő* (sparkling wine). True to its bistro aspirations, the daily specials are scribbled on the wall, in both Hungarian and English. V, Sas u. 17, tel. 1/311–0053. *Reservations essential. MC, V. Closed Sun.*

$$ CYRANO. ★ This smooth young bistro just off Vörösmarty tér has an arty, contemporary bent, with wrought-iron chairs, green-marble floors, and long-stem azure glasses. The creative kitchen sends out elegantly presented Hungarian and Continental dishes, from standards such as goulash and chicken paprikás to more eclectic tastes such as tender fried Camembert cheese with blueberry jam. V, Kristóf tér 7–8, tel. 1/266–3096. *Reservations essential. AE, DC, MC.*

$$ KISPIPA. This tiny, well-known restaurant with arched yellow-glass windows and piano bar is a favorite for both Budapest residents and passers-through. The kitchen delivers an expansive menu of first-rate Hungarian food; the venison ragout soup with tarragon is excellent. VII, Akácfa u. 38, tel. 1/342–2587. *Reservations essential. AE, MC. Closed Sun. and July–Aug.*

✓ **$ TÜKÖRY SÖRÖZŐ.** Hearty, decidedly nonvegetarian Hungarian fare comes in big portions at this popular spot close to Parliament. Best bets include pork cutlets stuffed with savory liver or apples and cheese, paired with a big mug of inexpensive beer. Courageous carnivores can sample the beefsteak tartare, topped with a raw egg. V, Hold u. 15, tel. 1/269–5027. *MC, V. Closed weekends.*

1,200
₤3·50

$ VISTA TRAVEL CAFÉ. ★ Opened in 1999 in a contemporary building just off Deák tér, this popular spot is an extension of the successful Vista travel agency complex down the street (☞ Contacts and Resources, *below*). Local regulars and visitors alike flock here for the affordable daily lunch menu and quiche specials. The menu is international, but Hungarian flags appear next to the local specialties—so you can try traditional *hortobágyi* (meat-filled) palacsinta and still get a chef salad. After you fill out your paper place mat rating the service and food, you can walk upstairs and check your e-mail at the Internet café. Note that there is a 3,000 Ft. minimum for credit card use. VII, *Paulay Ede u. 7, tel. 1/268 0888. AE, MC, V.*

NORTH BUDA

$$$$ VADRÓZSA. The "Wild Rose" always has fresh ones on the table; the restaurant is in a romantic old villa perched on a hilltop in the exclusive Rózsadomb district of Buda. It's elegant to the last detail, with white-glove service and piano music, and the garden is delightful in summer. Try the venison or grilled fish; the house specialty, grilled goose liver, is succulent perfection. II, *Pentelei Molnár u. 15, tel. 1/326–5817. Reservations essential. AE, DC, MC, V. Closed daily 4–7.*

$$$–$$$$ UDVARHÁZ. The views from this Buda hilltop restaurant are unsurpassed. As you dine indoors at tables set with white linens or outdoors on the open terrace, your meals are accompanied by vistas of the Danube bridges and Parliament far below. Excellent fresh fish is prepared tableside; you could also try veal and goose liver in paprika sauce, served with salty cottage cheese dumplings. Catering to the predominantly tourist crowd, folklore shows and live Gypsy music frequently enliven the scene. The buses up here are infrequent; it's easier to take a car or taxi. III, *Hármashatárhegyi út 2, tel. 1/388–6921. AE, DC, MC, V. Closed Mon. Nov.–Mar. No lunch weekdays Nov.–Mar.*

$$ NÁNCSI NÉNI. Aunt Nancy's restaurant is a perennial favorite,
★ despite its out-of-the-way location. Irresistibly cozy, the dining room feels like Grandma's country kitchen: Chains of paprika and garlic dangle from the low wooden ceiling above tables set with red-and-white gingham tablecloths and fresh bread tucked into tiny baskets. Shelves along the walls are crammed with jars of home-pickled vegetables, which you can purchase to take home. On the home-style Hungarian menu (large portions!) turkey

dishes manifest a creative flair, such as breast fillets stuffed with apples, peaches, mushrooms, cheese, and sour cream. Special touches include a popular outdoor garden in summer and free champagne for all couples in love. II, Ördögárok út 80, tel. 1/397–2742. Reservations essential July–Aug. AE, MC, V.

$ MARXIM. Two years after the death of socialism in Hungary, this simple pizza-and-pasta restaurant opened up to mock the old regime—and milk it for all it's worth. From the flashing red star above the door outside to the clever puns on the menus and photos of decorated hard-liners on the walls, the theme is "Communist nostalgia." Crowds of teenagers and blaring rock music make Marxim best suited for a lunch or snack. II, Kisrókus u. 23, tel. 1/212–4183. AE, DC, MC, V. No lunch Sun.

ÓBUDA

$$$ KÉHLI. This pricey but laid-back, sepia-tone neighborhood tavern is on a hard-to-find street near the Óbuda end of the Árpád Bridge. The food is hearty and heavy, just the way legendary Hungarian writer and voracious eater Gyula Krúdy (to whom the restaurant is dedicated) liked it when he lived in the neighborhood. Select from appetizers, such as hot bone marrow with garlic toast, before moving on to fried goose livers with mashed potatoes or turkey breast stuffed with cheese and goose liver. III, Mókus u. 22, tel. 1/250–4241 or 1/368–0613. AE, MC, V. No lunch weekdays.

$$$ KISBUDA GYÖNGYE. Considered one of the city's finest
★ restaurants, this intimate Óbuda restaurant is filled with antique furniture, and its walls are creatively decorated with an eclectic but elegant patchwork of carved wooden cupboard doors and panels. A violin-piano duo sets a romantic mood, and in warm weather you can dine outdoors in the cozy back garden. Try the venison with Transylvanian mushrooms or the popular liba lakodalmas (goose wedding feast), a roast goose leg, goose liver,

and goose cracklings. III, Kenyeres u. 34, tel. 1/368–6402 or 1/368–9246. Reservations essential. AE, DC, MC, V. Closed Sun.

TABÁN AND GELLÉRT HILL

$$ **TABÁNI KAKAS.** This popular restaurant just below Castle Hill has a distinctly friendly atmosphere and specializes in large helpings of poultry dishes, particularly goose. Try the catfish paprikás or the roast duck with steamed cabbage. I, Attila út 27, tel. 1/375–7165. AE, MC, V.

CITY PARK

$$$$ **GUNDEL.** George Lang, Hungary's best-known restaurateur, ★ showcases his native country's cuisine at this turn-of-the-20th-century palazzo. Dark-wood paneling, a dozen oil paintings by exemplary Hungarian artists, and tables set with Zsolnay porcelain make this the city's plushest, most handsome dining room. Violinist György Lakatos, of the legendary Lakatos Gypsy musician dynasty, strolls from table to table playing folk music, as waiters in black tie serve traditional favorites such as tender veal in a paprika-and-sour-cream sauce and carp Dorozsma (panfried with mushrooms). There's a large garden area where Sunday brunch is served in warm weather. XIV, Állatkerti út 2, tel. 1/321–3550. Reservations essential. Jacket and tie. AE, DC, MC, V. Closed daily 4–6.

$$$$ **ROBINSON RESTAURANT.** At this intimate dining room on the park's small lake, service is doting and the menu creative, with dishes such as crisp roast suckling pig with champagne-drenched cabbage or fresh fogas stuffed with spinach. Finish it off with a flaming cup of coffee Diablo, fueled with Grand Marnier. Padded pastel decor and low lighting wash the room in pleasant, if not Hungarian, elegance. XIV, Városliget, tel. 1/343–0955. Reservations essential. Jacket and tie. AE, DC, MC, V. Closed daily 4–6.

$$ BAGOLYVÁR. George Lang opened this restaurant next door to his gastronomic palace, Gundel (☞ *above*), in 1993. The informal yet polished dining room has a soaring wooden-beam ceiling, and the kitchen produces first-rate daily menus of home-style Hungarian specialties. Soups, served in shiny silver tureens, are particularly good. Musicians entertain with *cimbalom* (hammered dulcimer) music nightly from 7. In warm weather there is outdoor dining in a lovely back garden. *XIV, Állatkerti út 2,* tel. 1/343–0217. *AE, DC, MC, V.*

In This Chapter

Updated by Paul Olchváry

shopping

YOU'LL FIND PLENTY of expensive boutiques, folk-art and souvenir shops, foreign-language bookstores, and classical-record shops on or around touristy Váci utca, Budapest's famous, upscale pedestrian-only promenade. While a stroll along Váci utca is integral to a Budapest visit, browsing among some of the smaller, less touristy, more typically Hungarian shops in Pest—on the Kis körút (Little Ring Road) and Nagy körút (Great Ring Road)—may prove more interesting and less pricey. Lots of arty boutiques are springing up in the section of District V south of Ferenciek tere and toward the Danube, and around Kálvin tér. Falk Miksa utca, also in the fifth district, running south from Szent István körút, is one of the city's best antiques districts, lined on both sides with atmospheric little shops and galleries.

DEPARTMENT STORES AND MALLS

Skála Metro (VI, Nyugati tér 1–2, tel. 1/353–2222), opposite the Nyugati (West) Railroad Station, is one of the largest and best-known department stores, selling a little bit of not entirely everything. **Fontana** (Váci u. 16), has several floors of cosmetics, clothing, and other goods, all with price tags reflecting the store's expensive address. Pest's huge **Westend City Center** (VI, Váci út 1–3 [next to the Nyugati railroad station]), tel. 1/238–7777), and Buda's **Mammut** (II, Széna tér, tel. 1/345–8020), are just two of the many American-style malls that have sprung up in Hungary in recent years. They offer everything—except a genuine Hungarian atmosphere.

MARKETS

For true bargains and possibly an adventure, make an early morning trip to the vast **Ecseri Piac** (IX, Nagykőrösi út 156; take Bus 54 from Boráros tér), on the outskirts of the city. A colorful, chaotic market that shoppers have flocked to for decades, it is an arsenal of secondhand goods, where you can find everything from frayed Russian army fatigues to Herend and Zsolnay porcelain vases to antique silver chalices. Goods are sold at permanent tables set up in rows, from trunks of cars parked on the perimeter, and by lone, shady characters clutching just one or two items. As a foreigner, you may be overcharged, so prepare to haggle—it's part of the flea-market experience. Also, watch out for pickpockets. Ecseri is open weekdays 8–4, Saturday 8–3, but the best selection is on Saturday morning.

A colorful outdoor flea market is held weekend mornings from 7 to 2 at **Petőfi Csarnok** (XIV, Városliget, Zichy Mihály út 14, tel. 1/251–7266), in City Park. The quantity and selection are smaller than at Ecseri Piac, but it offers a fun flea-market experience closer to the city center. Many visitors buy red-star medals, Russian military watches, and other memorabilia from Communist days here. One other option is the **Vásárcsarnok** (☞ Downtown Pest and the Kis körút [Little Ring Road] in Here and There).

SPECIALTY STORES

Antiques

Falk Miksa utca (☞ *above*), lined with antiques stores, is a delightful street for multiple-shop browsing.

The shelves and tables at tiny **Anna Antikvitás** (V, Falk Miksa u. 18–20, tel. 1/302–5461) are stacked with exquisite antique textiles—from heavily embroidered wall hangings to dainty lace gloves. Exquisite cloth and lace parasols line the ceiling, but these, unfortunately, are not for sale; similar ones are, however, sometimes available. The store also carries assorted antique objets d'art. **BÁV Műtárgy** (V, Ferenciek tere 12, tel. 1/318–3381; V, Kossuth Lajos u. 1–3, tel. 1/318–6934; V, Szent István krt. 3, tel. 1/331–4534), the State Commission Trading House, has antiques of all shapes, sizes, kinds, and prices at its several branches around the city. While they all have a variety of objects, porcelain is the specialty at the branch on Kossuth Lajos utca, and paintings at the Szent István körút store. **Polgár Galéria és Aukciósház** (V, Kossuth Lajos u. 3, tel. 1/318–6954) sells everything from jewelry to furniture and also holds several auctions a year. **Qualitás** (V, Falk Miksa u. 32; V, Kígyó u. 5; VII, Dohány u. 1) sells paintings, furniture, and decorative objects at its branches around town.

Art Galleries

Budapest has dozens of art galleries showing and selling old works as well as the very latest. **Dovin Gallery** (V, Galamb u. 6, tel. 1/318–3673) specializes in Hungarian contemporary paintings. New York celebrity Yoko Ono opened **Gallery 56** (V, Falk Miksa u. 7, tel. 1/269–2529) to show art by internationally famed artists, such as Keith Haring, as well as works by up-and-coming Hungarian artists. You can also visit **Magyar Fotográfusok Háza** (☞ Andrássy út, in Here and There) for photography exhibits.

Books

You'll encounter bookselling stands throughout the streets and metro stations of the city, many of which sell English-language souvenir picturebooks at discount prices. **Váci utca** is lined with bookstores that sell glossy coffee-table books about Budapest and Hungary.

Atlantisz (V, Váci u. 31–33) has a selection of English classics, as well as academic texts. **Bestsellers** (V, Október 6 u. 11, tel. 1/312–1295) sells exclusively English-language books and publications, including best-selling paperbacks and a variety of travel guides about Hungary and beyond. The **Central European University**

Bookshop (V, Nádor u. 9, tel. 1/327–3096), in the Central European University, is a more academically focused branch of Bestsellers bookstore. If you're interested in reading up on this part of the world, this is the store for you. You'll also find a good selection of books in English at **Idegennyelvű Könyvesbolt** (V, Petőfi Sándor u. 2 [in Párizsi udvar]), which specializes in foreign-language books. **Írók boltja** (Writers' Bookshop; VI, Andrássy út 45, tel. 1/322–1645), one of Budapest's main literary bookstores, has a small but choice selection of Hungarian fiction and poetry translated into English. The hushed, literary atmosphere is tangible, and small tables are set out for reading and enjoying a cup of self-serve tea and coffee.

China, Crystal, and Porcelain

Hungary is famous for its age-old Herend porcelain, which is hand-painted in the village of Herend near Lake Balaton. For the Herend name and quality without the steep price tag, visit **Herend Village Pottery** (II, Bem rakpart 37, tel. 1/356–7899), where you can choose from Herend's practical line of durable ceramic cups, dishes, and table settings. The brand's largest Budapest store, **Herendi Porcelán Márkabolt** (V, József Nádor tér 11, tel. 1/317–2622), sells a variety of the delicate (and pricey) pieces, from figurines to dinner sets. Hungary's exquisite Zsolnay porcelain, created and hand-painted in Pécs, is sold at the **Zsolnay Márkabolt** (V, Kígyó u. 4, tel. 1/318–3712) and a few other locations.

Hungarian and Czech crystal is considerably less expensive here than in the United States. **Goda Kristály** (V, Váci u. 9, tel. 1/318–4630) has beautiful colored and clear pieces. **Haas & Czjzek** (VI, Bajcsy-Zsilinszky út 23, tel. 1/311–4094) has been in the business for more than 100 years, selling a variety of porcelain, glass, and ceramic pieces in traditional and contemporary styles. Crystal and porcelain dealers also sell their wares at the Ecseri Piac flea market (☞ Markets, *above*), often at discount prices, but those looking for authentic Herend and Zsolnay should beware of imitations.

Clothing

El Cabito (V, Múzeum krt. 35, tel. 318–8963), a tiny boutique across from the National Museum, offers cotton dresses of Hungarian and Far Eastern design—for reasonable prices. The **Hugo Boss Shop** (V, Aranykéz u. 2, tel. 318–3016), has a good selection of men's suits. High-fashion women's outfits by top Hungarian designers are for sale at **Monarchia** (V, Szabadsajtó út 6, tel. 1/318–3146), whose rich burgundy velvet draperies and ceilings are higher than its floor space. **Manier** (V, Váci u. 48 [entrance at Nyári Pál u. 4], tel. 1/318–1812) is a popular haute couture salon run by talented Hungarian designer Anikó Németh offering women's pieces ranging from quirky to totally outrageous. The store's second branch is across the street at Váci utca 53.

Folk Art

Handmade articles, such as embroidered tablecloths and painted plates, are sold all over the city by Transylvanian women wearing traditional scarves and colorful skirts. You can usually find them standing at **Moszkva tér, Jászai Mari tér,** outside the **Kossuth tér** metro, around **Váci utca,** and in the larger metro stations.

All types of folk art—pottery, blouses, jewelry boxes, wood carvings, embroidery—can be purchased at one of the many branches of Népművészet Háziipar, also called **Folkart Centrum** (V, Váci u. 14, tel. 1/318–5840), a large cooperative chain. Prices are reasonable, and selection and quality are good. **Holló Műhely** (V, Vitkovics Mihály u. 12, tel. 1/317–8103) sells the work of László Holló, a master wood craftsman who has resurrected traditional motifs and styles of earlier centuries. There are lovely hope chests, chairs, jewelry boxes, candlesticks, and more, all hand-carved and hand-painted with cheery folk motifs—a predominance of birds and flowers in reds, blues, and greens.

Home Decor and Gifts

Impresszió (V, Károly krt. 10, tel. 1/337–2772) is a little boutique packed with home-furnishings, baskets, picture frames, and decorative packaging, all made of natural materials and reasonably priced. The courtyard it calls home includes similar shops and a pleasant café. A few blocks away, just down the street from the Holló Műhely (☞ *above*), lies the **Interieur Stúdió** (V, Vitkovics Mihály u. 6, tel. 1/266–1666), offering wooden brushes, bookmarks, and even a birdcage; candles of all shapes and sizes; and sundry other objects for the home.

Music

Recordings of Hungarian folk music or of pieces played by Hungarian artists are widely available on compact discs, though cassettes and records are much cheaper and are sold throughout the city. CDs are normally quite expensive—about 4,000 Ft.

MCD Amadeus (V, Szende Pál u. 1, tel. 1/318–6691), just off the Duna korzó, has an extensive selection of classical CDs. **MCD Zeneszalon** (V, Vörösmarty tér 1, no phone) has a large selection of all types of music and is centrally located. Its separate, extensive section on Hungarian artists is great for gift- or souvenir-browsing. The **Rózsavölgyi Zenebolt** (V, Szervita tér 5, tel. 1/318–3500) is an old, established music store crowded with sheet music and largely classical recordings, but with other selections as well.

Toys

For a step back into the world before Pokemon cards and action figures, stop in at the tiny **Játékszerek Anno** (Toys Anno; VI, Teréz krt. 54, tel. 1/302–6234) store, where fabulous repros of antique European toys are sold. From simple paper puzzles to lovely stone building blocks to the 1940s wind-up metal monkeys on bicycles, these "nostalgia toys" are beautifully simple and exceptionally clever. Even if you're not a collector, it's worth a stop just to browse.

Wine

Stores specializing in Hungarian wines have become a trend in Budapest over the past few years. The best of them is the store run by the **Budapest Bortársaság** (Budapest Wine Society; I, Batthyány u. 59, tel. 1/212–2569 or 1/212–0262, fax 1/212–5285). The cellar shop at the base of Castle Hill always has an excellent selection of Hungary's finest wines, chosen by the wine society's discerning staff, who will happily help you with your purchases. Tastings are held Saturday from 2 to 6.

Updated by Paul Olchváry

outdoor activities and sports

IF YOU'RE FEELING ACTIVE even after exploring the city on foot, Budapest offers a wide selection of gyms and sports facilities, and a range of outdoor activities including golf and horseback riding.

Bicycling

Because of constant thefts, bicycle rentals are difficult to find in Hungary. **Bringóhintó**, a rental outfit on Margaret Island (Hajós Alfréd sétány 1, across from Thermal Hotel, tel. 1/329–2072), offers popular four-wheel pedaled contraptions called Bringóhintók, as well as traditional two-wheelers; standard bikes cost about 800 Ft. per hour or 1,500 Ft. until 8 AM the next day, with a 10,000 Ft. deposit. For more information about renting in Budapest, contact **Tourinform** (V, Sütő u. 2, tel. 1/317–9800). For brochures and general information on bicycling conditions and suggested routes, try Tourinform or contact the **Magyar Kerékpáros Túrázók Szövetsége** (Bicycle Touring Association of Hungary; V, Bajcsy-Zsilinszky út 31, 2nd floor, Apt. 3, tel. 1/332–7177).

Golf

Golf is still a new sport in Hungary, one that few Hungarians can afford. The closest place to putt is 35 km (22 mi) north of the city at the **Budapest Golfpark** (tel. 1/317–6025, 1/317–2749, or 06–26/392–463) in Kisoroszi. The park has an 18-hole, 72-par course and a driving range. Greens fees range from 7,000 Ft. to 8,000 Ft. Carts and equipment can be rented. The park is closed from about mid-November–mid-March.

Health and Fitness Clubs

Andi Stúdió (V, Hold u. 29, tel. 1/311–0740) is a trendy fitness club with adequate but sometimes overcrowded facilities. For about 650 Ft. you can work out on the weight machines (no real cardiovascular equipment to speak of) and sit in the sauna, or take an aerobics class, held every hour. **Gold's Gym** (VIII, Szentkirályi u. 26, tel. 1/267–4334) stands out as being the least cramped gym, with good weight-training and cardiovascular equipment and hourly aerobics classes in larger-than-usual spaces. A one-visit pass costs around 650 Ft.

Horseback Riding

Experienced riders can ride at the **Budapesti Lovas Klub** (Budapest Equestrian Club; VIII, Kerepesi út 7, tel./fax 1/313–5210) for about 1,500 Ft. per hour. Call about two weeks ahead to assure yourself a horse. In the verdant outskirts of Buda, the **Petneházy Lovas Centrum** (Petneházy Equestrian Center; 1029 Feketefej út 2, Adyliget, tel. 1/397–5048) offers horseback-riding lessons and trail rides for 1,800 Ft.–2,500 Ft. per hour. Note that English saddle, not Western, is the standard in Hungary.

Jogging

The path around the perimeter of **Margaret Island,** as well as the numerous pathways in the center, is level and inviting for a good run. **Városliget** (City Park) in flat Pest has paths good for jogging.

Spas and Thermal Baths

In addition to those listed below, newer, modern baths are open to the public at hotels, such as the **Danubius Grand Hotel Margitsziget** and the **Danubius Thermal Hotel Helia** (☞

Where to Stay). They lack the charm of their older peers but provide the latest treatments.

Gellért Thermal Baths (☞ Tabán and Gellért Hill, *in* Here and There); **Király Baths** (☞ North Buda, *in* Here and There); **Rác Baths** (☞ Tabán and Gellért Hill, *in* Here and There); **Rudas Baths** (☞ Tabán and Gellért Hill, *in* Here and There); **Széchenyi Baths** (☞ Városliget, *in* Here and There).

Tennis and Squash

On Margaret Island, **Euro-Gym Fitness Club** (XIII, Europa House, Margitsziget, tel. 1/339–8672) charges 700 Ft.–900 Ft. per hour to play on one of its eight clay courts; it's open from mid-April to mid-October, and you'll need to reserve a day or two in advance. **On-line Squash Club** (Budaörs, Forrás u. 8, tel. 23/501–2620), on the near outskirts of town, is a trendy full-facility fitness club with five squash courts. Hourly rates run 2,000 Ft.–2,800 Ft., depending on when you play. The club rents equipment and stays open until 11 PM on weekdays, 9 PM on weekends. **Városmajor Tennis Academy** (XII, Városmajor u. 63–69, tel. 1/202–5337) has five outdoor courts (clay and hexapet) available daily 7 AM–10 PM. They are lit for night play and covered by a tent in winter. Court fees run around 1,400 Ft. per hour in summer, 1,800 Ft.–3,000 Ft. in winter. Racket rentals and lessons are also offered. The Marriott Hotel's **World Class Fitness Center** (V, Apáczai Csere János u. 4, tel. 1/266–4290) has one excellent squash court available for 2,500 Ft.–4,500 Ft. an hour, depending on when you play; be sure to reserve it a day or two in advance.

In This Chapter

Updated by Paul Olchváry

nightlife and the arts

FOR THE LATEST ON ARTS EVENTS, consult the entertainment listings of the English-language press. Their entertainment calendars map out all that's happening in Budapest's arts and culture world— from thrash bands in wild clubs to performances at the Opera House. Another option is to stop in at the National Philharmonic ticket office (V, Mérleg u. 10, tel. 1/318–0281) and browse through the scores of free programs and fliers and scan the walls coated with upcoming concert posters. Hotels and tourist offices will provide you with a copy of the monthly publication *Programme*, which contains details of all cultural events.

As is the case in most other cities, the life of a club or disco in Budapest can be somewhat ephemeral. Those listed below are quite popular and seem to be here to stay. But for the very latest on the more transient "in" spots, consult the nightlife sections of the weekly *Budapest Sun* or *Budapest in Your Pocket*, published five times a year.

NIGHTLIFE

Budapest's nightlife is vibrant and diverse. For basic beer and wine drinking, *sörözős* and *borozós* (wine bars) abound, although the latter tend to serve the early-morning-spritzer-before-work types rather than nighttime revelers. For quiet conversation there are *drink-bárs* in most hotels and all over town, but beware of the inflated prices and steep cover charges. Cafés are preferable for unescorted women.

Most nightspots and clubs have bars, pool tables, and dance floors. Although some places do accept credit cards, it's best to expect to pay cash for your night on the town. Budapest also has its share of seedy go-go clubs and so-called "cabarets," some of which are known for scandalously excessive billing and physical intimidation. Be wary if you are "invited" in by women lingering nearby, and don't order anything without first seeing the price. What's more, in some pulsing nightspots it is not uncommon to find men weaving through the crowd selling drugs or themselves; the penalties for possessing even small amounts of illegal drugs are stiff.

A word of warning to the smoke-sensitive: Although a 1999 law requiring smoke-free areas in many public establishments has already had a discernible impact in restaurants, the bar scene is a firm reminder that Budapest remains a city of smokers. No matter where you spend your night out, chances are you'll come home smelling of cigarette smoke.

Bars and Clubs

Angel Bar and Disco (VII, Szövetség u. 33, tel. 1/351–6490) is one of Budapest's enduring and most popular gay bars (though all persuasions are welcome), with a rollicking dance floor. It's closed Monday–Wednesday.

Bahnhof (VI, Váci út 1, at Nyugati pu.) is, appropriately, in the Nyugati (West) train station and attracts swarms of young people to its large, crowded dance floor. The club hosts live bands and DJ'd music Wednesday–Saturday.

The most popular of Budapest's Irish pubs and a favorite expat watering hole is **Becketts** (V, Bajcsy-Zsilinszky út 72, tel. 1/311–1035), where Guinness flows freely and excellent Irish fare is served amid the gleams of polished wood and brass.

One of the city's hottest spots is **Café Capella** (V, Belgrád rakpart 23, tel. 1/318–6231), where a welcoming, gay-friendly crowd flocks to the glittery drag shows (held a few times a week) and revels to DJ'd club music until dawn.

A hip, mellow crowd mingles at the stylish **Cafe Incognito** (VI, Liszt Ferenc tér 3, tel. 1/351–9428), with low lighting and funky music kept at a conversation-friendly volume. Couches and armchairs in the back are comfy and private. It closes relatively early—at midnight.

Café Pierrot (I, Fortuna u. 14, tel. 1/375–6971), an elegant café and piano bar on a small street on Castle Hill, is well suited to a secret rendezvous.

With its abundance of soft chairs and changing exhibits of chic, abstract paintings, **Cafe Vian** (VI, Liszt Ferenc tér 9, tel. 1/342–8991) is the place to lounge about sipping cappuccino, beer, or a cocktail (non-alcoholic varieties available) while chatting, not to mention seeing and being seen. It closes at midnight.

Established Hungarian jazz headliners and young up-and-comers play Sunday–Tuesday in the popular if small, stylishly brick-walled **Fat Mo's** (VII, Nyári Pál u. 11, tel. 1/267–3199), which is open daily.

If crowds, low newspaper-mosaicked ceilings, and smoke-permeated air aren't your thing, avoid the **Old Man's Music Pub** (VII, Akácfa u. 13, tel. 1/322–7645). If hard-core live blues and friendly chaos *are*, don't miss out on the fun—complemented by a small dance floor.

Cool (and trendily dark) **Underground** (VI, Teréz krt. 30, tel. 1/311–1481) is below the artsy Művész movie theater. Exposed metal beams and girders and wackily shaped scrap-metal chairs and tables give this bar the requisite industrial look; the DJ spins progressive popular music. Weekends are packed with younger, sometimes rowdy, hipsters.

Casinos

Most of Budapest's 10 or so major casinos are open daily from 2 PM until 4 or 5 AM and offer gambling in hard currency—usually dollars—only.

The centrally located and popular **Las Vegas Casino** (V, Roosevelt tér 2, tel. 1/317–6022) is in the Hyatt Regency Hotel. In an 1879 building designed by prolific architect Miklós Ybl, who also designed the State Opera House, the **Várkert Casino** (I, Miklós Ybl tér 9, tel. 1/202–4244) is the most visually striking of the city's casinos.

THE ARTS

Tickets for arts events can be bought at the venues themselves, but many ticket offices sell them without extra charge. Prices are still very low, so markups of even 30% shouldn't dent your wallet if you book through your hotel. Inquire at Tourinform (☞ Visitor Information, in Practical Information) if you're not sure where to go. Ticket availability depends on the performance and season—it's usually possible to get tickets a few days before a show, but performances by major international artists sell out early. Tickets to Budapest Festival Orchestra concerts and festival events also go particularly quickly.

Theater and opera tickets are sold at the **Central Theater Booking Office** (VI, Andrássy út 18, tel. 1/312–0000). For classical concert, ballet, and opera tickets, as well as tickets for major pop and rock shows, go to the **National Philharmonic Ticket Office** (☞ *above*). **Music Mix Ticket Service** (V, Váci utca 33, tel. 1/317–7736) specializes in popular music but handles other genres as well.

Classical Music and Opera

The tiny recital room of the **Bartók Béla Emlékház** (Bartók Béla Memorial House; II, Csalán út 29, tel. 1/394–4472) hosts intimate Friday evening chamber music recitals by well-known ensembles from mid-March to June and September to mid-December.

The **Budapest Kongresszusi Központ** (Budapest Convention Center; XII, Jagelló út 1–3, tel. 1/209–1990) is the city's largest-capacity (but least atmospheric) classical concert venue and usually hosts the largest-selling events of the Spring Festival.

The homely little sister of the Opera House, the **Erkel Színház** (Erkel Theater; VII, Köztársaság tér 30, tel. 1/333–0540) is Budapest's other main opera and ballet venue. There are no regular performances in the summer.

Liszt Ferenc Zeneakadémia (Franz Liszt Academy of Music; VI, Liszt Ferenc tér 8, tel. 1/342–0179), usually referred to as the Music Academy, is Budapest's premier classical concert venue, hosting orchestra and chamber music concerts in its splendid main hall. It's sometimes possible to grab a standing-room ticket just before a performance here.

The glittering **Magyar Állami Operaház** (Hungarian State Opera House; VI, Andrássy út 22, tel. 1/331–2550), Budapest's main venue for operas and classical ballet, presents an international repertoire of classical and modern works as well as such Hungarian favorites as Kodály's *Háry János*. Except during the one-week BudaFest international opera and ballet festival in mid-August, the Opera House is closed during the summer.

Colorful operettas such as those by Lehár and Kálmán are staged at their main Budapest venue, the **Operetta Theater** (VI, Nagymező u. 19, tel. 1/353–2172); also look for modern dance productions and Hungarian renditions of popular Broadway classics.

Classical concerts are held regularly at the **Pesti Vigadó** (Pest Concert Hall; V, Vigadó tér 2, tel. 1/318–9167).

English-Language Movies

Many of the English-language movies that come to Budapest are subtitled in Hungarian rather than dubbed; this applies less so, however, to independent and art films. There are more than 30 cinemas that regularly show films in English, and tickets are very inexpensive by Western standards (400–700 Ft.). Consult the movie matrix in the *Budapest Sun* for a weekly list of what's showing.

Folk Dancing

Many of Budapest's district cultural centers regularly hold traditional regional folk-dancing evenings, or dance houses (*táncház*), often with general instruction at the beginning. These sessions provide a less touristy way to taste Hungarian culture.

Almássy téri Szabadidő központ (Almássy Square Recreation Center; VII, Almássy tér 6, tel. 1/352–1572) holds numerous folk-dancing evenings, representing Hungarian as well as Greek and other ethnic cultures. Traditionally the wildest *táncház* is held Saturday night at the **Belvárosi Ifjúsági ház** (City Youth Center; V, Molnár u. 9, tel. 1/317–5928), where the stomping and whirling go on way into the night; the center, like many such venues, closes from mid-July to mid-August. A well-known Transylvanian folk ensemble, Tatros, hosts a weekly dance house at the **Marczibányi téri Művelődési ház** (Marczibányi tér Cultural Center; II, Marczibányi tér 5/a, tel. 1/212–5789), usually on Wednesday night.

Folklore Performances

The **Hungarian State Folk Ensemble** performs regularly at the **Budai Vigadó** (I, Corvin tér 8, tel. 1/201–3766); shows incorporate instrumental music, dancing, and singing.

The **Folklór Centrum** (XI, Fehérvári út 47, tel. 1/203–3868) has been a major venue for folklore performances for more than 30 years. It hosts regular traditional folk concerts and dance performances from spring through fall.

Theaters

The **Madách Theater** (VII, Erzsébet krt. 31–33, tel. 1/478–2041) produces colorful musicals in Hungarian, including a popular adaptation of *Cats*. For English-language dramas check out the **Merlin Theater** (V, Gerlóczy u. 4, tel. 1/317–9338). Another musical theater is the **Thália Theater** (VI, Nagymező u. 22–24, tel. 1/331–0500). The sparkling **Vígszínház** (Comedy Theater; XIII, Pannónia u. 1, tel. 1/329–2340) hosts classical concerts and dance performances but is primarily a venue for musicals, such as the Hungarian adaptation of *West Side Story*.

In This Chapter

Updated by Paul Olchváry

side trips
from budapest

ABOUT 40 KM (25 MI) NORTH of Budapest, the Danube abandons its eastward course and turns abruptly south toward the capital, cutting through the Börzsöny and Visegrád hills. This area is called the Danube Bend and includes the Baroque town of Szentendre, the hilltop castle ruins and town of Visegrád, and the cathedral town of Esztergom. The most scenically varied part of Hungary, the region is home to a chain of riverside spas and beaches, bare volcanic mountains, and limestone hills. Here, in the heartland, are the traces of the country's history—the remains of the Roman Empire's frontier, the battlefields of the Middle Ages, and the relics of the Hungarian Renaissance.

The west bank of the Danube is the more interesting side, with three engaging and picturesque towns—Szentendre, Visegrád, and Esztergom. The district can be covered by car in one day, the total round-trip no more than 112 km (70 mi), although this affords only a cursory look. A day trip to Szentendre while based in Budapest plus two days for Visegrád and Esztergom, with a night in either (both have lovely small hotels), would be best.

On the Danube's eastern bank, Vác is the only larger town of any real interest. No bridges span the Danube in this region, but there are numerous ferries (between Visegrád and Nagymaros, Basaharc and Szob, Szentendre Island and Vác), making it possible to combine a visit to both sides of the Danube on the same excursion.

Though the Danube Bend's west bank contains the bulk of historical sights, the less-traveled east bank has the excellent hiking trails of the Börzsöny mountain range, which extends along the Danube from Vác to Zebegény before curving toward the Slovak border. The Pilis and Visegrád hills on the Danube's western side and the Börzsöny Hills on the east are popular nature escapes.

Work had started on a hydroelectric dam near Nagymaros, across from Visegrád, in the mid-1980s. The project was proposed by Austria and what was then Czechoslovakia, and reluctantly agreed to by Hungary, but protests from the Blues (Hungary's equivalent of Germany's Greens), coupled with rapid democratization, succeeded in halting the project and rescuing a region of great natural beauty. This seemed to come undone in 1998: the International Court in the Hague ruled that the original agreement between what is now Slovakia and Hungary was still valid, and the two countries signed a preliminary agreement to start building a dam after all in the coming years. However, diplomatic foot-dragging and friendlier bilateral relations have so far precluded the reemergence of any project like that which had prompted the tensions in the first place.

Numbers in the margin correspond to numbers on the Danube Bend map.

SZENTENDRE

★ ⑤④ *21 km (13 mi) north of Budapest.*

A romantic little town with a lively atmosphere and a flourishing artists' colony, this is the highlight of the Danube Bend. With its profusion of enchanting church steeples, colorful Baroque houses, and winding, narrow cobblestone streets, it's no wonder Szentendre attracts swarms of visitors, tripling its population in peak season.

Szentendre was first settled by Serbs and Greeks fleeing the advancing Turks in the 16th and 17th centuries. They built

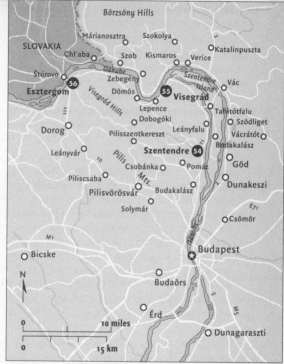

houses and churches in their own style—rich in reds and blues seldom seen elsewhere in Hungary. To truly savor Szentendre, duck into any and every cobblestone side street that appeals to you. Baroque houses with shingle roofs (often with an arched eye-of-God upstairs window) and colorful stone walls will enchant your eye and pique your curiosity.

Fő tér is Szentendre's main square, the centerpiece of which is an ornate **Memorial Cross** erected by Serbs in gratitude because the town was spared from a plague. The cross has a crucifixion painted on it and stands atop a triangular pillar adorned with a dozen icon paintings.

Every house on Fő tér is a designated landmark, and three of them are open to the public: the **Ferenczy Múzeum** (Ferenczy Museum) at No. 6, with paintings of Szentendre landscapes; the **Kmetty Múzeum** (Kmetty Museum) at No. 21, with works by János Kmetty, a pioneer of Hungarian avant-garde painting; and the **Szentendrei Képtár** (Municipal Gallery) at Nos. 2–5, with an excellent collection of local contemporary art and international changing exhibits. *Each museum 150 Ft. Wed.–Sun. 10–4.*

Gracing the corner of Görög utca (Greek Street) and Szentendre's main square, Fő tér, the so-called **Görög templom** (Greek Church, also known as Blagovestenska Church) is actually a Serbian Orthodox church that takes its name from the Greek inscription on a red-marble gravestone set in its wall. This elegant edifice was built between 1752 and 1754 by a rococo master, Andreas Mayerhoffer, on the site of a wooden church dating to the Great Serbian Migration (around 690). Its greatest glory—a symmetrical floor-to-ceiling panoply of stunning icons—was painted between 1802 and 1804 by Mihailo Zivkovic, a Serbian painter from Buda. *Görög u. at Fő tér. 100 Ft. Mar.–Oct., Tues.–Sun. 10–5.*

If you have time for only one of Szentendre's myriad museums, ★ don't miss the **Kovács Margit Múzeum,** which displays the collected works of Budapest ceramics artist Margit Kovács, who died in 1977. She left behind a wealth of richly textured work that ranges from ceramics to life-size sculptures. Admission to the museum is limited to 15 persons at a time, so it is wise to line up early or at lunchtime, when the herds of tour groups are occupied elsewhere. *Vastagh György u. 1 (off Görög u.), tel. 26/310–244 ext. 114. 300 Ft. Mid-Mar.–early Oct., daily 10–6; early Oct.–mid-Mar., Tues.–Sun. 10–4. www.pmmi.hu*

Perched atop Vár-domb (Castle Hill) is Szentendre's oldest surviving monument, the **Katolikus plébánia templom** (Catholic Parish Church), dating to the 13th century. After many reconstructions, its oldest visible part is a 15th-century sundial in the doorway. The church's small cobblestone yard hosts an arts-and-crafts market and, often on weekends in summer, street entertainment. From here, views over Szentendre's angular tile rooftops and steeples and of the Danube beyond are superb. *Vár-domb. Free. Hrs vary; check with Tourinform (☞ Visitor Information, below).*

★ The **Szerb Ortodox Egyházi Gyüjtemény** (Serbian Orthodox Collection of Religious Art) displays exquisite artifacts relating to the history of the Serbian Orthodox Church in Hungary. Icons, altars, robes, 16th-century prayer books, and a 17th-century cross with (legend has it) a bullet hole through it were collected from all over the country, after being sold or stolen from Serbian churches that were abandoned when most Serbs returned to their homeland at the turn of the 20th century and following World War I. The museum shares a tranquil yard with the imposing Serbian Orthodox Cathedral. *Pátriárka u. 5, tel. 26/312–399. 100 Ft. May–Sept., Tues.–Sun. 10–6; Oct.–Dec. and Mar.–Apr., Tues.–Sun. 10–4; Jan.–Feb., Fri.–Sun. 10–4.*

The crimson steeple of the handsome **Szerb Ortodox Bazilika** (Serbian Orthodox Cathedral) presides over a restful tree-shaded yard crowning the hill just north of Vár-domb (Castle Hill). It was built in the 1740s with a much more lavish but arguably less beautiful iconostasis than is found in the Greek Church below it. *Pátriárka u. 5, tel. 26/312–399. Hrs vary; check with Tourinform (☞ Visitor Information, below) or Serbian Orthodox Collection of Religious Art museum officials.*

NEED A BREAK? For a quick cholesterol boost, grab a floppy, freshly fried *lángos* (flat, salty fried dough) drizzled with sour cream or brushed with garlic at **Piknik Büfé** (Dumtsa Jenő u. 22), just next door to the Tourinform office.

Szentendre's farthest-flung museum is the **Szabadtéri Néprajzi Múzeum** (Open-Air Ethnographic Museum), the largest open-air museum in the country. It is a living re-creation of 18th- and 19th-century village life from different regions of Hungary—the sort of place where blacksmith shops and a horse-powered mill compete with wooden houses and folk handicrafts for your attention. During regular crafts demonstrations, visitors can sit back and watch or give it a try themselves. Five kilometers (3 mi) to the northwest, the museum is reachable by bus from the Szentendre terminus of the HÉV suburban railway. *Szabadságforrás út, tel. 26/312–304. About 300 Ft. Apr.–Oct., Tues.–Sun. 10–5.*

Where to Stay and Eat

$$$ RÉGIMÓDI. This upstairs restaurant with fine wines and game specialties is practically on Fő tér. Lace curtains and antique knickknacks give the small dining room a homey intimacy. The summer terrace is a delightful place to dine alfresco and look out over the red-tile rooftops. *Dumtsa Jenő u. 2, tel. 26/311–105. AE, DC, MC, V.*

$$ ARANYSÁRKÁNY. On the road up to the Serbian Orthodox ★ Cathedral, the Golden Dragon lies in wait with seven large tables, which you share with strangers on a busy night. The delicious food is prepared in a turbulent open kitchen, but all the activity is justified by the cold cherry soup with red wine or the hot *sárkány erőleves* (Dragon Bouillon) with quail eggs and vegetables. Try the smoked goose liver with rose petal jam; the "opium" pudding (custard with lots of poppy seeds mixed in), with its "poison green" (i.e., kiwi) sauce, is also recommended. Wash it down with one of 75 varieties of Hungarian wine. *Alkotmány u. 1/a, tel. 26/311–670. AE, DC, MC, V.*

$$ RAB RÁBY. Fish soup and fresh grilled trout are the specialties in
★ this extremely popular, friendly restaurant with rustic wood beams
and myriad old instruments, lanterns, cowbells, and other eclectic
antiques. *Péter Pál u. 1, tel. 26/310–819. Reservations essential July–
Aug. MC, V.*

$$ VIDÁM SZERZETESEK. The Happy Monks opened as a family
restaurant, though in recent years it has become something of a
tourist haunt; the reasonably priced menu is, after all, in 20
languages. The atmosphere is casual and decidedly cheerful; the
food is typically Hungarian: heavy, hearty, and delicious. Try the
Suhajda (hat soup), a savory brew of smoked meat topped with a
tasty dough cap baked over the bowl. *Bogdányi út 3–5, tel. 26/310–
544. AE, MC, V. Closed Mon.*

$$ BÜKKÖS PANZIÓ. Just west of the main square and across the
bridge over tiny Bükkös Brook, this neat, well-run inn is one of
the most conveniently located hotels in the village. The narrow
staircase and small rooms give it a homey feel. *Bükkös part 16, H-
2000, tel. 26/312–021, tel./fax 26/310–782. 16 rooms. Restaurant,
laundry service. MC, V. www.hotels.hu/bukkos*

$$ KENTAUR HÁZ. This handsome, modern, chalet-style hotel is a
two-minute walk from Fő tér, on what may be Hungary's last
surviving square still to bear Karl Marx's name. Rooms are clean
and simple, with pale-gray carpeting, blond unfinished-wood
paneling, and pastel-pink walls hung with original paintings by
local artists. Upstairs rooms are sunniest and most spacious.
*Marx tér 3–5, H-2000, tel./fax 26/312–125. 16 rooms. Bar, breakfast
room. No credit cards. www.hotels.hu/kentaur*

$$ ST. ANDREA PANZIÓ. This remodeled *panzió* (pension) atop a
grassy incline has all the makings of a Swiss chalet. Attic space
has been converted into modernized rooms with clean tile showers.
On a warm day you can eat breakfast on the outside patio. The
owners are very friendly; they've even been known to specially cook
meals for guests arriving late at night. *Egres u. 22, H-2000, tel./fax*

26/311–989. 16 rooms, 2 suites. Restaurant. No credit cards.
www.hotels.hu/st_andrea

Outdoor Activities and Sports

BICYCLING

The waterfront and streets beyond Szentendre's main square are perfect for a bike ride—free of jostling cobblestones and relatively calm and quiet. Check with Tourinform (☞ Visitor Information, *below*) for local rental outfits. Rentals are available in Budapest (☞ Outdoor Activities and Sports); bicycles are permitted in a designated car of each HÉV suburban railway train. Many people make the trip between Budapest and Szentendre on bicycle along the designated bike path, which runs on busy roads in some places but is pleasant and separate from the road for the stretch between Békásmegyer and Szentendre.

Nightlife and the Arts

Most of Szentendre's concerts and entertainment events occur during the spring and summer. For current schedules and ticket information, contact **Tourinform** (☞ Visitor Information, *below*).

The annual **Spring Festival,** usually held from mid-March through early April, offers classical concerts in some of Szentendre's churches, as well as jazz, folk, and rock performances in the cultural center and other venues about town. In July, the **Szentendre Summer Days** festival brings open-air theater performances and jazz and classical concerts to Fő tér and the cobblestone courtyard fronting the town hall. Although the plays are usually in Hungarian, the setting alone can make it an enjoyable experience.

Shopping

Flooded with tourists in summer, Szentendre is saturated with the requisite **souvenir shops.** Among the attractive but overpriced goods sold in every store are dolls dressed in traditional folk costumes, wooden trinkets, pottery, and colorful hand-embroidered tablecloths, doilies, and blouses. The best bargains are the hand-embroidered blankets and bags sold by dozens of elderly women in traditional folk attire, who stand for hours on the town's crowded streets. (Because of high weekend traffic, most Szentendre stores stay open all day on weekends, unlike those in Budapest. Galleries are closed Monday and accept major credit cards, although other stores may not.)

The one tiny room of **art-éria galéria** (Városház tér 1, tel. 26/310–111) is crammed with paintings, graphics, and sculptures by 21 of Szentendre's best contemporary artists.

Topped with an abstract-statue trio of topless, pale-pink and baby-blue women in polka-dot bikini panties, the **Christoff Galéria** (Bartók Béla u. 8, tel. 26/317–031) is hard to miss as you climb the steep hill to its door. The gallery sells works by local and Hungarian contemporary artists, including those of popular visual artist and musician ef Zambo, creator of its crowning females. It's best to call ahead to check opening times.

The **Gallery Erdész** (Bercsényi u. 4, tel. 26/317–925) displays an impressive selection of contemporary Hungarian art, as well as gifts such as leather bags, colored glass vases, and handmade paper—not to mention some unique, curvaceous silver pieces made by a famous local jeweler.

Beautiful stationery, booklets, and other handmade paper products are displayed and sold at the **László Vincze Paper Mill** (Angyal u. 5, tel. 26/314–328). In this small workshop at the top of a broken cobblestone street, Mr. Vincze lovingly creates his thick, watermarked paper, using traditional, 2,000-year old bleaching methods.

The sophisticated **Erdész Galéria** (Fő tér 20, tel. 26/310–139), on Szentendre's main square (not to be confused with the Gallery

Erdész, *above*), displays paintings, statues, and other works by some 30 local artists.

Péter-Pál Galéria (Péter-Pál u. 1, tel. 26/311–182) has a good selection of handmade textiles, wrought-iron work, glass, and ceramics.

VISEGRÁD

55 *23 km (14 mi) north of Szentendre.*

Visegrád was the seat of the Hungarian kings during the 14th century, when a fortress built here by the Angevin kings became the royal residence. Today, the imposing fortress at the top of the hill towers over the peaceful little town of quiet, tree-lined streets and solid old houses. The forested hills rising just behind the town offer popular hiking possibilities. For a taste of Visegrád's best, climb to the Fellegvár, and wander and take in the views of the Danube curving through the countryside; but make time to stroll around the village center a bit—on Fő utca and other streets that pique your interest.

★ Crowning the top of a 1,148-ft hill, the dramatic **Fellegvár** (Citadel) was built in the 13th century and served as the seat of Hungarian kings in the early 14th century. In the Middle Ages, the citadel was where the Holy Crown and other royal regalia were kept, until they were stolen by a dishonorable maid of honor in 1440; 23 years later, King Matthias had to pay 80,000 Ft. to retrieve them from Austria. (For the time being, the crown is safe in the Parliament building in Budapest.) A *panoptikum* (akin to slide projection) show portraying the era of the kings is included free with admission. The breathtaking views of the Danube Bend below are ample reward for the strenuous, 40-minute hike up. *tel. 26/398–101. 250 Ft. Mid-Mar.–mid-Nov., daily 9–5; mid-Nov.–mid-Mar., weekends 10–dusk; closed in snowy conditions.*

In the 13th–14th centuries, King Matthias Corvinus had a separate palace built on the banks of the Danube below the citadel. It was eventually razed by the Turks, and not until 1934 were the ruins finally excavated. Nowadays you can see the disheveled remnants of the **Királyi palota** (Royal Palace) and its **Salamon torony** (Salomon Tower), referred to together as the **Mátyás Király Múzeum** (King Matthias Museum). The Salomon Tower houses two small exhibits displaying ancient statues and well structures from the age of King Matthias. Especially worth seeing is the red-marble well, built by a 15th-century Italian architect. Above a ceremonial courtyard rise the palace's various halls; on the left you can still see a few fine original carvings, which give an idea of how magnificent the palace must once have been. Inside the palace is a small exhibit on its history, as well as a collection of gravestones dating from Roman times to the 19th century. Fridays in May, the museum hosts medieval-crafts demonstrations. *Fő u. 23, tel. 26/398–026. Royal Palace 300 Ft., Salomon Tower 200 Ft. Royal Palace: Tues.–Sun. 9–4:30; Salomon Tower: May–Sept., Tues.–Sun. 9–4:30.*

OFF THE BEATEN PATH **MILLENNIAL CHAPEL** – Like a tiny precious gem, the miniature chapel sits in a small clearing, tucked away on a corner down Fő utca, Visegrád's main street. The bite-size, powder-yellow church was built in 1896 to celebrate the Magyar Millennium and is open only on Pentecost and a few other holidays. *Fő u. 113.*

Where to Stay and Eat

$$ **GULYÁS CSÁRDA.** This cozy little restaurant, decorated with ★ antique folk art and memorabilia, complements its eight indoor tables with additional seating outside during the summer. The cuisine is typical home-style Hungarian, with a limited selection of tasty traditional dishes. Try the halászlé served in a pot and kept warm on a small spirit burner. *Nagy Lajos király u. 4, tel. 26/398–329. MC, V.*

$$ **SIRÁLY RESTAURANT.** Right across from the ferry station, the airy Seagull Restaurant is justifiably well regarded for its rolled fillet of venison and its many vegetarian dishes, including fried soy steak with vegetables. In summer, when cooking is often done on the terrace overlooking the Danube, expect barbecued meats and stews, soups, and gulyás served in old-fashioned pots. *Rév u. 15, tel. 26/398–376. AE, MC, V. Closed Nov.–Feb.*

$ **FEKETE HOLLÓ.** The popular "Black Raven" restaurant has an elegant yet comfortable atmosphere—a great place for a full meal or just a beer. Try the chef's creative specialties, such as coconut chicken leg with pineapples, or stick to such regional staples as fresh, grilled fish; either way save room for the palacsinta with nuts and chocolate. *Rév út 12, tel. 26/397–289. No credit cards. Closed Nov.–Mar.*

$$$ **BETA HOTEL SILVANUS.** Set high up on Fekete Hill, this hotel is renowned for its spectacular views. Rooms are bright and clean, with simple furnishings, and offer a choice of forest or Danube (about 1,000 Ft. more expensive) views. Since it's at the end of a steep, narrow road, the Silvanus is recommended for motorists (although a bus does stop nearby) and hikers or bikers—there are linking trails in the forest behind. *Fekete-hegy, H-2025, tel./fax 26/398–311). 88 rooms, 5 suites. Restaurant, bar, café, pub, indoor pool, sauna, bowling, mountain bikes. AE, DC, MC, V. www.danubiusgroup.com/silvanus*

$ **HOTEL & HAUS HONTI.** A newly opened, 21-room hotel and its older, alpine-style sibling pension share the same yard in a quiet residential area, a three-minute walk from the town center. Apple trees and a gurgling brook render a peaceful, rustic ambience. The pension has seven tiny, clean rooms tucked under sloping ceilings and with balconies, some with lovely Danube views; the rooms in the hotel are more spacious and a tad more expensive, some with balconies affording a splendid view of the Citadel in the distance. Breakfast costs about $4 more per room. *Fő u. 66, H-2025, tel. 26/398–120. 28 rooms. No credit cards.*

Nightlife and the Arts

The **Visegrád International Palace Games,** held annually on the second weekend in July, take the castle complex back to its medieval heyday, with horseback jousting tournaments, archery games, a medieval music and crafts fair, and other festivities. Contact Visegrád Tours (☞ Visitor Information, *below*) for specifics.

Outdoor Activities and Sports

HIKING

Visegrád makes a great base for exploring the trails of the Visegrád and Pilis hills. A hiking map is posted on the corner of Fő utca and Rév utca, just above the pale-green Roman Catholic Parish Church. A well-trodden, well-marked hiking trail (posted with red signs) leads from the edge of Visegrád to the town of Pilisszentlászló, a wonderful 8½-km (5⅓ mi (about three-hour)) journey through the oak and beech forests of the Visegrád Hills into the Pilis conservation region. Deer, wild boars, and mouflons roam freely here, and there are fields of yellow-blooming spring pheasant's eye and black pulsatilla.

SWIMMING

The outdoor thermal pools at **Lepence,** 3 km (2 mi) southwest of Visegrád on route 11, combine good soaking with excellent Danube Bend views. *Lepence-völgyi Termál és Strandfürdő, Lepence,* tel. 26/398–208. 400 Ft. May–Sept., daily 9–6:30.

TOBOGGAN SLIDE

🐌 Winding through the trees on Nagy-Villám Hill is the **Wiegand Toboggan Run,** one of the longest slides you've ever seen. You ride on a small cart that is pulled uphill by trolley, then careen down the slope in a small, steel trough that resembles a bobsled run. *Panoráma út, ½ km (¼ mi) from Fellegvár,* tel. 26/397–397. 180 Ft. weekdays, 220 Ft. weekends and holidays; 1,000 Ft. for six runs weekdays, 1,200 Ft. weekends and holidays. May–Sept., daily 10–7; Apr. and Oct., daily 11–4; Nov.–Mar. (weather permitting), weekends 11–4.

ESZTERGOM

56 *21 km (13 mi) north of Visegrád.*

Esztergom stands on the site of a Roman fortress, at the westernmost curve of the heart-shape Danube Bend, where the Danube marks the border between Hungary and Slovakia. (The bridge that once joined these two countries was destroyed by the Nazis near the end of World War II, though parts of the span can still be seen.) St. Stephen, the first Christian king of Hungary and founder of the nation, was crowned here in the year 1000, establishing Esztergom as Hungary's first capital, which it remained for the next 250 years. The majestic Bazilika, Hungary's largest, is Esztergom's main draw, followed by the fine art collection of the Primate's Palace. If you like strolling, leave yourself a little time to explore the narrow streets of Viziváros (Watertown) below the Bazilika, lined with brightly painted Baroque buildings.

★ Esztergom's **Bazilika** (cathedral), the largest in Hungary, stands on a hill overlooking the town; it is now the seat of the cardinal primate of Hungary. It was here, in the center of Hungarian Catholicism, that the famous anti-Communist cleric, Cardinal József Mindszenty, was finally reburied (he'd had to be buried in Austria when he died in 1975) in 1991 ending an era of religious intolerance and prosecution and a sorrowful chapter in Hungarian history. Its most interesting features are the Bakócz Chapel (1506), named for a primate of Hungary who only narrowly missed becoming pope; and the sacristy, which contains a valuable collection of medieval ecclesiastical art. If your timing is lucky, you could attend a concert during one of the various classical music festivals held here in summer (☞ Nightlife and the Arts). *Szent István tér, tel. 33/311–895. Free. Apr.–late Oct., daily 7–4; late Oct.–Mar., weekdays 7–4, weekends 7–5.*

Considered by many to be Hungary's finest art gallery, the **Keresztény Múzeum** (Museum of Christian Art), in the Primate's Palace, has a thorough collection of early Hungarian and Italian paintings (the 14th- and 15th-century Italian collection is unusually large for a museum outside Italy). Unique holdings include the *Coffin of Our Lord* from Garamszentbenedek (today Hronský Benádik, Slovakia); the wooden statues of the Apostles and of the Roman soldiers guarding the coffin are masterpieces of Hungarian Baroque sculpture. The building also holds the Primate's Archives, which contain 20,000 volumes, including several medieval codices. Permission to visit the archives must be obtained in advance. *Primate's Palace: Mindszenty tér 2, tel. 33/ 413–880. 200 Ft. Mid-Mar.–Sept., Tues.–Sun. 10–6; Jan.–mid-Mar., Tues.–Sun. 10–5.*

To the south of the cathedral, on **Szent Tamás Hill**, is a small church dedicated to St. Thomas à Becket of Canterbury. From here you can look down on the town and see how the Danube temporarily splits, forming an island, **Prímás-sziget**, that locals use as a base for waterskiing and swimming, in spite of the pollution. To reach it, cross the Kossuth Bridge.

Where to Stay and Eat

$$ PRIMÁSPINCE. Arched ceilings and exposed brick walls make a charming setting for refined Hungarian fare at this touristy but good restaurant just below the cathedral. Try the tournedos Budapest style (tender beef with sautéed vegetables and paprika) or the thick turkey breast Fiaker style (stuffed with ham and melted cheese). *Szent István tér 4, tel. 33/313–495. AE, DC, MC, V. No dinner Jan.–Feb.*

$–$$ SZALMA CSÁRDA & PANZIÓ. A short drive or five-minute walk from the center of town onto Prímás-sziget takes you to the Hay Inn and Pension, in a tranquil setting on this fairly undeveloped stretch of the Danube. The restaurant is splendidly rustic, with strings of dried paprika hanging from the ceiling and an earthenware stove the size of a baby elephant in the main room. Listen to live Gypsy music while enjoying "long-forgotten peasant dishes"—actually, typical meals such as chicken paprika which, with wax beans and dill-spiced dumplings on the side, are apparently prepared the way they used to be, down on the farm. The 20-room pension, which from the outside resembles a ranch house, opened in 2000 right next door and is run by the same family. While the cramped rooms, with low, summer-camp-like pinewood beds, are not for those who prefer such amenities as TVs and phones, they are clean and bright. *Nagy-Duna sétány 2, on Prímás-sziget, H-2500, tel./fax 33/315–336 or 33/403–838. No credit cards.*

$$ ALABÁRDOS PANZIÓ. Conveniently located downhill from the cathedral, this cozy, remodeled home provides excellent views from upstairs. Rooms (doubles and quads) are small but less cramped than at other small pensions. Breakfast is included. *Bajcsy-Zsilinszky u. 49, H-2500, tel./fax 33/312–640. 22 rooms. Breakfast room. No credit cards.*

$$ HOTEL ESZTERGOM. Simply furnished and sports-oriented, this hotel has a good location on Prímás-szíget. Tennis, swimming, bowling, horseback riding, and water-sports facilities are nearby. All rooms have balconies; the largest, and nicest, rooms face away from the river. *Prímás-szíget, Nagy Duna Sétány, H-2500, tel. 33/412–883, fax 33/412–853. 34 rooms, 2 suites. Restaurant, meeting room. AE, DC, MC, V. www.danubiusgroup.com/esztergom*

$$ RIA PANZIÓ. In this small, friendly guest house near the cathedral, all of the small, no-frills rooms face a garden courtyard. *Batthyány u. 11–13, H-2500, tel. 33/313–115. 13 rooms. Breakfast room. AE, MC, V. www.hotels.hu/ria_panzio*

Nightlife and the Arts

Every two years Esztergom hosts the **Nemzetközi Gitár Fesztivál** (International Guitar Festival) during which renowned classical guitarists from around the world hold master classes and workshops for participants. Recitals are held nearly every night in Esztergom's **Zöldház Művelődési Központ** (Green House Cultural Center) or the **Tanítóképző Főiskola** (Teachers College), where the festival is based, or elsewhere in Budapest and neighboring towns. The climax of it all is the glorious closing concert, held in the basilica, in which the hundreds of participants join together and perform as a guitar orchestra. The festival runs for two weeks, usually beginning in early August; the next one will be held in 2001. Tickets and information are available at the tourist offices.

DANUBE BEND A TO Z
Arriving and Departing

BY BOAT

If you have enough time, you can travel to the west-bank towns by boat from Budapest, a leisurely and pleasant journey, especially in summer and spring. Boating from Budapest to Esztergom takes about five hours, to Visegrád about three hours. Boats leave from the main Pest dock at Vigadó tér. The disadvantage of boat travel is that a round-trip by slow boat doesn't allow much time for sightseeing; the Esztergom route, for example, allows only under two hours before it's time to head back. Many people head upriver by boat in the morning and back down by bus or train as it's getting dark. There is daily service from Budapest to Visegrád, stopping in Szentendre. Contact **MAHART Tours** (tel. 1/484–4013 or 318–1223) in Budapest for complete schedule information.

BY BUS

Buses run regularly between Budapest's Árpád híd bus station and most towns along both sides of the Danube. The ride to Szentendre takes about half an hour.

BY CAR

Route 11 runs along the western shore of the Danube, connecting Budapest to Szentendre, Visegrád, and Esztergom.

BY TRAIN

Esztergom has a frequent daily express and local train service to and from Budapest's Nyugati (West) Station. Trains do not run to Visegrád. The **HÉV** suburban railway runs between Batthyány tér (or Margaret Island, one stop north) in Budapest and Szentendre about every 10–20 minutes daily; the trip takes 40 minutes and a *kiegészítő* (supplementary) ticket—which you need in addition to a Budapest public transport pass or ticket—costs around 170 Ft. one-way.

Getting Around

BY BICYCLE

The Danube Bend is a great place to explore by bike; most towns are relatively close together. Some routes have separate bike paths, while others run along the roads. Consult the "Danube Bend Cyclists' Map" (available at tourist offices) and Tourinform (☞ Visitor Information, *below*) for exact information.

BY BOAT

Boat travel along the river is slow and scenic. **MAHART**'s (☞ *above*) boats ply the river between Budapest and Esztergom, Szentendre, and Visegrád. You can plan your sightseeing to catch a boat connection from one town to the other (☞ Arriving and Departing, *above*).

BY BUS

Buses are cheap and relatively comfortable—if you get a seat, as opposed to standing for an hour or more; they link all major towns along both banks. If you don't have a car, this is the best way to get around, since train service is spotty.

BY FERRY

As there are no bridges across the Danube in this region, there is regular daily passenger and car **ferry service** between several points on opposite sides of the Danube (except in winter when the river is too icy). The crossing generally takes about 10 minutes and costs roughly 600 Ft. per car and driver, 120 Ft. per passenger. The crossing between Nagymaros and Visegrád is recommended, as it affords gorgeous views of Visegrád's citadel and includes a beautiful drive through rolling hills on Route 12 south and then west of Nagymaros. Contact the relevant tourist office (☞ Visitor Information, *below*) for schedule details.

BY TRAIN

Train travel in the region is difficult; Visegrád has no train service and there are no direct connections between Szentendre and Esztergom.

Contacts and Resources

EMERGENCIES

Ambulance (tel. 104). **Fire** (tel. 105). **Police** (tel. 107).

GUIDED TOURS

IBUSZ Travel (tel. 1/485–2762 or 1/317–7767) organizes daylong bus trips from Budapest along the Danube, stopping in Esztergom, Visegrád, and Szentendre on Tuesday, Friday, and Sunday from May through October, and Saturday only from November through April. There's commentary in English; the cost, including lunch and admission fees, is about 16,000 Ft.

Cityrama (in Budapest, tel. 1/302–4382) runs its popular "Danube Tour" (approximately 16,000 Ft.) daily Wednesday–Sunday from May until September. Departing from Budapest, the full-day tour begins with sightseeing in Visegrád, then Esztergom. After lunch, the tour moves on to Szentendre for a guided walk and makes a scenic return to Budapest down the Danube. (The tour returns by bus when the water level is low and in winter, when the tour is offered once a week; call ahead for exact dates and times.)

Your checklist for a perfect journey

WAY AHEAD
- Devise a trip budget.
- Write down the five things you want most from this trip. Keep this list handy before and during your trip.
- Make plane or train reservations. Book lodging and rental cars.
- Arrange for pet care.
- Check your passport. Apply for a new one if necessary.
- Photocopy important documents and store in a safe place.

A MONTH BEFORE
- Make restaurant reservations and buy theater and concert tickets. Visit fodors.com for links to local events.
- Familiarize yourself with the local language or lingo.

TWO WEEKS BEFORE
- Replenish your supply of medications.
- Create your itinerary.
- Enjoy a book or movie set in your destination to get you in the mood.

- Develop a packing list. Shop for missing essentials. Repair and launder or dry-clean your clothes.

A WEEK BEFORE
- Stop newspaper deliveries. Pay bills.
- Acquire traveler's checks.
- Stock up on film.
- Label your luggage.
- Finalize your packing list— take less than you think you need.
- Create a toiletries kit filled with travel-size essentials.
- Get lots of sleep. Don't get sick before your trip.

A DAY BEFORE
- Drink plenty of water.
- Check your travel documents.
- Get packing!

DURING YOUR TRIP
- Keep a journal/scrapbook.
- Spend time with locals.
- Take time to explore. Don't plan too much.

VISITOR INFORMATION

Budapest: Tourinform (V, Sütő u. 2, tel. 1/317–9800).
Esztergom: Grantours (Széchenyi tér 25, tel./fax 33/413–756);
IBUSZ (Kossuth L. u. 5, tel. 33/412–552); **Komtourist** (Lőrinc u.
6, tel. 33/312–082). **Szentendre: Tourinform** (Dumtsa Jenő u.
22, tel. 26/317–965 or 26/317–966). **Visegrád: Visegrád Tours**
(Sirály Restaurant, Rév u. 15, tel. 26/398–160).

Updated by Betsy Maury

where to stay

BUDAPEST IS WELL EQUIPPED with hotels and hostels, but the increase in tourism since 1989 has put a strain on the city's often crowded lodgings. Advance reservations are strongly advised, especially at the lower-price hotels. Many of the major luxury and business-class hotel chains are represented in Budapest; however, all of them are Hungarian-run franchise operations with native touches that you won't find in any other Hilton or Marriott.

In winter it's not difficult to find a hotel room, even at the last minute, and prices are usually reduced by 20%–30%. By far the cheapest and most accessible beds in the city are rooms ($20–$25 for a double room) in private homes. Although most tourist offices book private rooms, the supply is limited, so try to arrive in Budapest early in the morning.

Addresses below are preceded by the district number (in Roman numerals) and include the Hungarian postal code. Districts V, VI, and VII are in downtown Pest; I includes Castle Hill, the main tourist district of Buda.

CATEGORY	BUDAPEST*
$$$$	over $200
$$$	$140–$200
$$	$80–$140
$	under $80

All prices are for a standard double room with bath and breakfast during peak season (June through August).

$$$$ ART'OTEL. A short walk up the Danube from the Chain Bridge, this hip new boutique hotel is the first of its kind in Budapest. Like its sibling properties in Berlin and Dresden, the hotel-cum-gallery is dedicated to the work of a single artist, American Donald Sultan. From the carpets to the paintings, the china to the water fountains, the entire hotel is decorated with Sultan's designs, amounting to a multimillion-dollar collection of his art. Chic contemporary furniture contrasts elegantly with restored original moldings and doorframes in the older buildings' rooms. I, Bem rakpart 16–19, H-1011, tel. 1/487–9487, fax 1/487–9488. 156 rooms, 9 suites. Restaurant, café, air-conditioning, in-room data ports, no-smoking rooms, beauty salon, sauna, meeting rooms, parking (fee). AE, DC, MC, V. www.parkplazaww.com

$$$$ BUDAPEST HILTON. Built in 1977 around a 13th-century monastery adjacent to the Matthias Church, this perfectly integrated architectural wonder overlooks the Danube from the choicest site on Castle Hill. Every contemporary room has a remarkable view; Danube vistas cost more. Children, regardless of age, get free accommodation when sharing a room with their parents. Breakfast is not included in room rates. I, Hess András tér 1–3, H-1014, tel. 1/488–6600; 800/445–8667 in the U.S. and Canada; fax 1/488–6644. 295 rooms, 26 suites. 3 restaurants, 2 bars, café, air-conditioning, in-room data ports, beauty salon, sauna, exercise room, dry cleaning, laundry service, business services, meeting rooms, travel services, parking (free and fee). AE, DC, MC, V. www.hilton.com

$$$$ BUDAPEST MARRIOTT. In this sophisticated yet friendly hotel on the Danube in downtown Pest, attention to detail is evident, from the buffet of pastries served daily in the lobby to the feather-light ring of the front-desk bell. Guest rooms have lush carpets, floral bedspreads, and etched glass. The layout takes advantage of the hotel's prime Danube location, offering breathtaking views of Gellért Hill, the Chain and Elizabeth bridges, and Castle Hill — even from the impressive healthclub. V, Apáczai Csere János u. 4, H-1052, tel. 1/266–7000; 800/831–4004 in the U.S. and Canada; fax 1/266–5000. 362 rooms, 11 suites. 3 restaurants, bar, air-conditioning, in-

room data ports, no-smoking rooms, health club, squash, shops, baby-sitting, dry cleaning, laundry service, business services, meeting rooms, travel services, parking (fee). AE, DC, MC, V. www.marriott.com

$$$$ DANUBIUS HOTEL GELLÉRT. ★ The double-deck rotunda of this grand Hungarian spa hotel leads you to expect a string orchestra playing "The Emperor Waltz." Built in 1918, the Jugendstil Gellért was favored by Otto von Hapsburg, son of the last emperor. Rooms range from palatial suites to tiny spaces. Now part of the Danubius hotel chain, the Gellért has begun an ambitious overhaul, refurnishing all rooms in the mood of the original Jugendstil style. Inquire about completed rooms when you reserve. The best views—across the Danube or up Gellért Hill—are more expensive; avoid those that face the building's inner core. If you're planning a weekend trip well in advance, inquire about special packages; the prices can be more friendly. The monumental, ornate thermal baths in the hotel's spa are its pièce de résistance. Admission to the spa is free to hotel guests (medical treatments cost extra). XI, *Gellért tér 1, H-1111, tel. 1/385–2200, fax 1/466–6631. 220 rooms, 13 suites. Restaurant, bar, brasserie, café, no-smoking rooms, indoor pool, beauty salon, spa, mineral baths, baby-sitting, business services, meeting rooms, parking (fee). AE, DC, MC, V. www.danubiusgroup.com*

$$$$ HOTEL INTER-CONTINENTAL BUDAPEST. Formerly the Fórum Hotel, this modern, riverside hotel consistently wins applause for its gracious appointments and excellent service. Sixty percent of the rooms have river views (these are more expensive); rooms on higher floors ensure the least noise. The hotel café, Corso Bar, is locally known for its pastries. Breakfast is not included in the room rates. V, *Apáczai Csere János u. 12–14, Box 231, H-1368, tel. 1/327–6333, fax 1/327–6357. 398 rooms, 16 suites. 2 restaurants, bar, café, air-conditioning, in-room data ports, no-smoking floors, pool, health club, business services, meeting rooms, car rental, parking (fee). AE, DC, MC, V. www.interconti.com*

$$$$ HYATT REGENCY BUDAPEST. ★ The spectacular 10-story interior—a mix of glass capsule elevators, cascading tropical greenery, an

art'otel, 3

Astoria, 16

Budapest Hilton, 4

Budapest Marriott, 15

Carlton Hotel, 7

Citadella, 10

Danubius Grand Hotel Margitsziget, 1

Danubius Hotel Gellért, 11

Danubius Thermal Hotel Helia, 2

Flamenco, 9

Hotel Benczúr, 19

Hotel Inter-Continental Budapest, 13

Hyatt Regency Budapest, 12

Kempinski Hotel Corvinus Budapest, 14

Kulturinov, 5

Mercure Hotel Budapest Nemzeti, 17

Molnár Panzió, 8

Radisson SAS Béke, 18

Victoria, 6

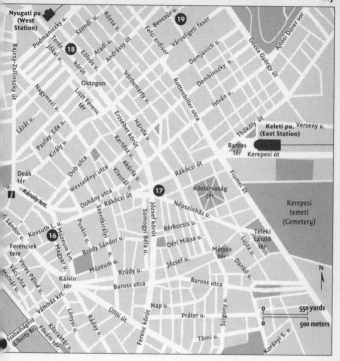

Nyugati pu.
(West
Station)

Podmaniczky u.

Szondi u.

Rózsa u.

Teréz
körút

Aradi u.

Benczúr u.

19

Felsö erdösor

Városligeti fasor

Bajcsy-Zsilinszky út

Jókai u.

Eötvös u.

Andrássy út

18

Damjanich u.

Dózsa György út

Ajtósi Dürer sor

Nagymező u.

Oktogon

Vörösmarty u.

Dembinszky u.

Lázár u.

Liszt Ferenc
tér

Rottenbiller utca

István u.

Paulay Ede u.

Erzsébet körút

Hársfa u.

Thököly út

Keleti pu.
(East Station)

Verseny u.

Király u.

Kertész u.

Baross
tér

Kerepesi út

Deák
tér

Dob utca

Wesselényi utca

Akácfa u.

Klauzál u.

Rákóczi út

Fiumei út

i

Károly krt.

Dohány utca

Rákóczi út

17

Köztársaság
tér

Kerepesi
temeti
(Cemetery)

n Sándor u.

Kossuth L. u.

Szentkirályi

Puskin u.

16

Múzeum krt.

Magyar u.

József körút

Somogyi Béla u.

Népszínház u.

Bérkocsis u.

Déri Miksa u.

Teleki
László
tér

Lujza u.

Ferenciek
tere

Reáltanoda u.

Bródy Sándor u.

Mátyás
tér

Dankó u.

Váci utca

Molnár u.

Kálvin
tér

Múzeum u.

Krúdy u.

József u.

Baross utca

Baross utca

N

Vámház krt.

Nap u.

Práter u.

Szigony u.

0   550 yards

Szabadság híd
(Liberty Bri)

Közraktár u.

Lónyai u.

Ráday u.

Üllői út

Ferenc körút

Tömö u.

0   500 meters

Fövám tér

Korányi S. u.

open bar, and café—is surpassed only by the views across the Danube to Castle Hill (rooms with a river view cost substantially more). Rooms are classy, in muted blues and light woods. V, Roosevelt tér 2, H-1051, tel. 1/266–1234, fax 1/266–9101. 330 rooms, 23 suites. 3 restaurants, 2 bars, air-conditioning, in-room data ports, no-smoking rooms, indoor pool, beauty salon, sauna, exercise room, casino, solarium, business services, meeting rooms, travel services, parking (fee). AE, DC, MC, V. www.hyatt.com

$$$$ **KEMPINSKI HOTEL CORVINUS BUDAPEST.** This sleek luxury
★ hotel is the favored lodging of visiting VIPs—from rock superstars to business moguls. Unlike those of other nearby hotels, rooms are spacious, with blond and black Swedish geometric inlaid woods and an emphasis on functional touches, such as three phones in every room, and large, sparkling bathrooms. The hotel's business services stand out as the city's best. Breakfast is not included in the room rates. V, Erzsébet tér 7–8, H-1051, tel. 1/429–3777; 800/426–3135 in the U.S. and Canada; fax 1/429–4777. 342 rooms, 27 suites. 2 restaurants, bar, lobby lounge, pub, shopping arcade, air-conditioning, in-room data ports, no-smoking rooms, indoor pool, barbershop, beauty salon, massage, health club, shops, dry cleaning, laundry service, business services, meeting rooms, travel services, parking (fee). AE, DC, MC, V. www.kempinski-budapest.com

$$$ **DANUBIUS GRAND HOTEL MARGITSZIGET.** Built in 1873, this venerable hotel is part of the Danubius hotel chain. Rooms have high ceilings and old-fashioned trimmings—down comforters and ornate chandeliers. Because it's connected to a bubbling thermal spa next door and is located on car-free Margaret Island in the Danube right between Buda and Pest, the Danubius Grand feels removed from the city but is still only a short taxi or bus ride away. XIII, Margit-sziget, H-1138, tel. 1/329–2300; 1/349–2769 (reservations); fax 1/329–3923 (reservations), 1/329–2429 (reception). 164 rooms, 10 suites. 2 restaurants, no-smoking rooms, indoor pool, beauty salon, massage, sauna, spa, mineral baths, exercise room, bicycles, meeting rooms, travel services, free parking. AE, DC, MC, V. www.danubiusgroup.com

ONE LAST TRAVEL TIP:

Pack an easy way to reach the world.

123 456 7891 2345
J.D. SMITH

Wherever you travel, the MCI WorldCom Card℠ is the easiest way to stay in touch. You can use it to call to and from more than 125 countries worldwide. And you can earn bonus miles every time you use your card. So go ahead, travel the world. MCI WorldCom℠ makes it even more rewarding. For additional access codes, visit **www.wcom.com/worldphone**.

MCI WORLDCOM.

EASY TO CALL WORLDWIDE

1. Just dial the WorldPhone® access number of the country you're calling from.

2. Dial or give the operator your MCI WorldCom Card number.

3. Dial or give the number you're calling.

Belgium ◆	0800-10012
Czech Republic ◆	00-42-000112
Denmark ◆	8001-0022

France ◆	0-800-99-0019
Germany	0800-888-8000
Hungary ◆	06▼-800-01411
Ireland	1-800-55-1001
Italy ◆	172-1022
Mexico	01-800-021-8000
Netherlands ◆	0800-022-91-22
Spain	900-99-0014
Switzerland ◆	0800-89-0222
United Kingdom	0800-89-0222
United States	1-800-888-8000

◆ Public phones may require deposit of coin or phone card for dial tone.   ▼ Wait for second dial tone.

EARN FREQUENT FLIER MILES

Bureau de change

Cambio

外国為替

In this city, you can find money on almost any street.

NO-FEE FOREIGN EXCHANGE

The Chase Manhattan Bank has over 80 convenient
locations near New York City destinations such as:

> Times Square
> Rockefeller Center
> Empire State Building
> 2 World Trade Center
> United Nations Plaza

Exchange any of 75 foreign currencies

 CHASE

THE RIGHT RELATIONSHIP IS EVERYTHING.®

$$$ DANUBIUS THERMAL HOTEL HELIA. A sleek Scandinavian design and less hectic location upriver from downtown make this spa hotel on the Danube a change of pace from its Pest peers. Guests can be in town in minutes or take advantage of the thermal baths and special health packages—including everything from Turkish baths to electrotherapy and fitness tests. Most of the comfortable rooms have Danube views. XIII, Kárpát u. 62–64, H-1133, tel. 1/452–5800; fax 1/452–5801. 254 rooms, 8 suites. Restaurant, bar, café, indoor pool, beauty salon, hot tub, massage, sauna, spa, steam room, mineral baths, tennis courts, exercise room, business services, meeting rooms, free parking. AE, DC, MC, V.

$$$ RADISSON SAS BÉKE. The well-situated Béke has a glittering turn-of-the-20th-century facade, a lobby lined with mosaics and statuary, and bellmen bowing before the grand marble staircase. Guest rooms resemble solidly modern living rooms, with two-tone wood furnishings and pastel decor. VI, Teréz krt. 43, H-1067, tel. 1/301–1600, fax 1/301–1615. 238 rooms, 8 suites. 2 restaurants, 2 bars, café, air-conditioning, in-room data ports, no-smoking rooms, pool, beauty salon, sauna, solarium, business services, meeting rooms, travel services, parking (fee). AE, DC, MC, V.

$$ ASTORIA. This turn-of-the-20th-century hotel that remains an oasis of quiet in hectic surroundings. Staff members are always—but unobtrusively—on hand. Rooms are genteel, spacious, and comfortable, and rather like Grandma's sitting room, in Empire style with an occasional antique. The Astoria's vintage Café Mirror is a wonderful place to relive the Hungarian coffeehouse tradition. V, Kossuth Lajos u. 19–21, H-1053, tel. 1/317–3411, fax 1/318–6798. 125 rooms, 5 suites. Restaurant, bar, café, no-smoking rooms, nightclub, business services, meeting rooms, free parking. AE, DC, MC, V.

$$ HOTEL BENCZÚR. Escape to this quiet hotel in the leafy embassy district off Andrássy út. Rooms here are well-equipped, with minibars and modern phones, though the furnishings are quite plain. The proximity to outdoor restaurants and bars make this hotel an attractive option. The Benczúr shares the building with Hotel Pedagógus. VI, Benczúr u. 35, H-1068, tel. 1/342–7970, fax 1/342–1558. 93 rooms. Restaurant, no-smoking rooms, meeting room, free parking. MC, V.

$$ CARLTON HOTEL. Tucked behind an alleyway at the foot of Castle Hill, this modern property (formerly named the Alba Hotel) is a short walk via the Chain Bridge from lively business and shopping districts. Rooms are clean and quiet, with white-and-pale-gray contemporary decor. I, Apor Péter u. 3, H-1011, tel. 1/224–0999 or 1/375–8658, fax 1/224–0990. 95 rooms. Bar, breakfast room, air-conditioning, no-smoking rooms, meeting room, parking (fee). AE, DC, MC, V. www.hotels.hu/carlton

$$ FLAMENCO. Classy though sometimes overlooked, this hotel in the Buda foothills is a welcome addition to this side of the river. A wall of windows in the low-ceiling lobby opens out onto views of a park. Service is professional, and the rooms are above average in this price category. XI, Tas Vezér u. 7, H-1113, tel. 1/372–2165 or 1/372–2000, fax 1/372–2100. 352 rooms, 8 suites. 2 restaurants, indoor pool, beauty salon, sauna, solarium, business services, meeting rooms, travel services, parking (fee). AE, DC, MC, V.

$$ MERCURE HOTEL BUDAPEST NEMZETI. With a lovely, baby-blue Baroque facade, the Nemzeti reflects the grand mood of the turn of the 20th century. Many of the rooms have pretty furnishings and air-conditioning; be sure to ask for one of these rooms ($10 extra) for optimal comfort. The hotel is located at bustling Blaha Lujza tér in the center of Pest, which tends toward the seedy after dark; although windows are double-paned, to ensure a quiet night, ask for a room facing the inner courtyard. VIII, József krt. 4, H-1088, tel. 1/303–9310, fax 1/314–0019, tel./fax 1/303–9162. 75 rooms, 1 suite. Restaurant, piano bar, air-conditioning, meeting room, travel services. AE, DC, MC, V. www.hungary.com/pannonia/nemzeti

$$ MOLNÁR PANZIÓ. This immaculate guest house nestled high above Buda on Széchenyi Hill has clean and bright rooms with pleasant wood paneling and pastel-color modern furnishings; most have distant views of Castle Hill and Gellért Hill, and some have balconies. Eight rooms in a newer addition next door are more private and have superior bathrooms. XII, Fodor u. 143, H-1124, tel. 1/395–1873, tel./fax 1/395–1872. 23 rooms. Restaurant, bar, sauna, exercise room, playground, travel services, free parking. AE, DC, MC, V. www.hotel-molnar.hu

$$ VICTORIA. ★ The Parliament building and city lights twinkling over the river can be seen from the picture windows of every room at this establishment right on the Danube. The tiny hotel mixes the charm of a small inn with the modern comforts of a business hotel. The location—an easy walk from Castle Hill sights and downtown Pest—couldn't be better. I, Bem rakpart 11, H-1011, tel. 1/457–8080, fax 1/457–8088. 27 rooms, 1 suite. Bar, air-conditioning, sauna, meeting room, travel services, parking (fee). AE, DC, MC, V. www.victoria.hu

$ CITADELLA. Comparatively basic, the Citadella is nevertheless very popular for its price and for its stunning location—right inside the fortress. Half of the rooms compose a youth hostel; none have bathrooms, but half have showers. Breakfast is not included in the rates. XI, Citadella sétány, Gellérthegy, H-1118, tel. 1/466–5794, fax 1/386–0505. 20 rooms, none with bath. Breakfast room. No credit cards.

$ KULTURINOV. ★ One wing of a magnificent 1902 neo-Baroque castle now houses basic budget accommodations. Rooms come with two or three beds and are clean and have showers but no tubs. In one of Budapest's most famous squares in the luxurious castle district. I, Szentháromság tér 6, H-1014, tel. 1/355–0122 or 1/375–1651, fax 1/375–1886. 16 rooms. Snack bar, library, meeting rooms. AE, DC, MC, V.

PRACTICAL INFORMATION

Air Travel to and from Budapest

BOOKING

When you book **look for nonstop flights** and **remember that "direct" flights stop at least once.** Try to avoid connecting flights, which require a change of plane.

CARRIERS

In most cases, flights from the United States on major U.S. airlines have a European co-carrier that provides a connecting flight from a gateway in Europe. Some European national airlines offer nonstop service from the United States to their own countries as well as connecting flights; others only provide connections within Europe.

The most convenient way to fly between Hungary and the United States is with **Malév Hungarian Airlines** nonstop direct service between JFK International Airport in New York and Budapest's Ferihegy Airport—the only nonstop flight that exists. All are on roomy Boeing 767-200s and take approximately nine hours. The service runs daily most of the year.

Malév and other national airlines fly nonstop from most European capitals. **British Airways** (tel. 1/318–3299 or 1/266–6699) and Malév offer daily nonstop service between Budapest and London.

➤ MAJOR AIRLINES: **Continental** (tel. 800/231–0856). **Delta** (tel. 800/241–4141). **Northwest** (tel. 800/447–4747). **United** (tel. 800/538–2929).

➤ NATIONAL AIRLINES WITH SERVICE FROM U.S.: Hungary: **Malév Hungarian Airlines** (tel. 212/757–6446, in Budapest, tel. 1/235–3535; 06/40–212–121 toll free; 1/235–3804 [ticketing]; tel. 1/296–9696 [after-hours flight information]).

CHECK-IN & BOARDING

Assuming that not everyone with a ticket will show up, airlines routinely overbook planes. When everyone does, airlines ask for volunteers to give up their seats. In return, these volunteers usually get a certificate for a free flight and are rebooked on the next flight out. If there are not enough volunteers, the airline must choose who will be denied boarding. The first to get bumped are passengers who checked in late and those flying on discounted tickets, so **get to the gate and check in as early as possible,** especially during peak periods.

Always **bring a government-issued photo I.D. to the airport.** You may be asked to show it before you are allowed to check in.

CUTTING COSTS

The least expensive airfares to Budapest must usually be purchased in advance and are non-refundable. —the same fare may not be available the next day. Always **check different routings** and look into using different airports. Travel agents, especially low-fare specialists (☞ Discounts & Deals, *below*), are helpful.

Consolidators are another good source. They buy tickets for scheduled international flights at reduced rates from the airlines, then sell them at prices that beat the best fare available directly from the airlines, usually without restrictions. Sometimes you can even get your money back if you need to return the ticket. Carefully read the fine print detailing penalties for changes and cancellations, and **confirm your consolidator reservation with the airline.**

➤ CONSOLIDATORS: **Cheap Tickets** (tel. 800/377–1000). **Discount Airline Ticket Service** (tel. 800/576–1600). **Unitravel** (tel. 800/325–2222). **Up & Away Travel** (tel. 212/889–2345). **World Travel Network** (tel. 800/409–6753).

HOW TO COMPLAIN

If your baggage goes astray or your flight goes awry, complain right away. Most carriers require that you **file a claim** **immediately.**

➤ AIRLINE COMPLAINTS: U.S. Department of Transportation **Aviation Consumer Protection Division** (C-75, Room 4107, Washington, DC 20590, tel. 202/366–2220, www.dot.gov/airconsumer). **Federal Aviation Administration Consumer Hotline** (tel. 800/322–7873).

Airports & Transfers

Ferihegy Repülőtér, Hungary's only commercial airport with regularly scheduled service, is 24 km (15 mi) southeast of downtown Budapest. All non-Hungarian airlines operate from Terminal 2B; those of Malév, from Terminal 2A. (A note of clarification should you run into some confusion: The older part of the airport, Terminal 1, no longer serves commercial flights; and so the main airport is now often referred to as "Ferihegy 2," and the terminals as simply "A" and "B.")

➤ AIRPORT INFORMATION: **Ferihegy Repülőtér** (Ferihegy Airport) (tel. 1/296–9696 or for same-day flight information; 1/296–8000 for arrivals, 1/296–7000 for departures; 1/296–8108 for lost & found).

AIRPORT TRANSFERS

Many hotels offer their guests car or minibus transportation to and from Ferihegy, but all of them charge for the service. You should arrange for a pickup in advance. If you're taking a taxi, allow 40 minutes during nonpeak hours and at least an hour during rush hours (7 AM–9 AM from the airport, 4 PM–6 PM from the city). Official **Airport Taxis** are queued at the exit and overseen by a taxi monitor; rates are fixed according to the zone of your final destination. A taxi ride to the center of Budapest will cost around 4,500 Ft. Trips to the airport are about 3,500 Ft. from Pest, 4,000 Ft. from Buda. Avoid taxi drivers who approach you before you are out of the arrivals lounge.

LRI Centrum Bus minibuses run every half hour from 5:30 AM to 9:30 PM to and from the Hotel Kempinski on Erzsébet tér (near the main bus station and the Deák tér metro hub) in downtown Budapest. It takes almost the same time as taxis but costs only about 700 Ft. The **LRI Airport Shuttle** provides convenient door-to-door service between the airport and any address in the city. To get to the airport, call to arrange a pickup; to get to the city, make arrangements at LRI's airport desk. Service to or from either terminal costs around 1,500 Ft. per person; since it normally shuttles several people at once, remember to allow time for a few other pickups or dropoffs.

➤ TAXIS & SHUTTLES: **Airport Taxis** (tel. 1/282–2222). **LRI Airport Shuttle** (tel. 1/296–8555 or 1/296–6283). **LRI Centrum Bus** (tel. 1/296–8555 or 1/296–6283).

Boat & Ferry Travel

From late July through early September, two swift hydrofoils leave Vienna daily at 8 AM and 1 PM (once-a-day trips are scheduled mid-April–late July and September–late October). After a 5½-hour journey downriver, with a stop in the Slovak capital, Bratislava, and views of Hungary's largest church, the cathedral in Esztergom, the boats head into Budapest via its main artery, the Danube. The upriver journey takes about an hour longer. The cost is 780 AS one-way.

➤ BOAT & FERRY INFORMATION: For reservations and information in Budapest, call **MAHART Tours** (tel. 1/484–4025; 1/484–4010; 43–1/729–2161; 43–1/729–2162 in Vienna).

Bus Travel around Budapest

Trams (villamos) and buses (autóbusz) are abundant and convenient. One fare ticket (95 Ft.; valid on all forms of public transportation) is valid for only one ride in one direction. Tickets cannot be bought on board; they are widely available in metro stations and newsstands and must be validated on board by inserting them downward facing you into the little devices provided for that purpose, then pulling the knob. Alternatively, you can purchase a *napijegy* (day ticket, 740 Ft.; a three-day "tourist ticket" costs 1,500 Ft.), which allows unlimited travel on all services within the city limits. Hold on to whatever ticket you have; spot-checks by aggressive undercover checkers (look for the red armbands) are numerous and often targeted at tourists. Trolley-bus stops are marked with red, rectangular signs that list the route stops; regular bus stops are marked with similar light blue signs. (The trolley-buses and regular buses themselves are red and blue, respectively.) Tram stops are marked by light blue or yellow signs. Most lines run from 5 AM and stop operating at 11 PM, but there is all-night service on certain key routes. Consult the separate night-bus map posted in most metro stations for all-night service.

Bus Travel to and from Budapest

Unless you latch onto a real deal on airfare, a bus ticket from London's Victoria Terminal (tel. 0171/730–0202) is probably the cheapest transit from the United Kingdom to Budapest, although it may take a little research, as regularly scheduled routes to most cities in Eastern and Central Europe are practically nonexistent. Check newspaper ads for eastbound passage.

Long-distance buses link Budapest with most cities in Hungary. Services to the eastern part of the country leave from the **Népstadion station** (tel. 1/485–2100). For the Danube Bend, buses leave from the bus terminal at **Árpád Bridge** (tel. 1/329–1450). Arrive at least 20 minutes before departure to buy a ticket (this is not possible for all routes, as tickets for some routes can only be purchased directly from the driver); and if there's a crowd pressing to get on, feel free to wave your pre-purchased ticket about as you jostle your way aboard (technically speaking, reserved seats must be occupied by no later than ten minutes before departure time).

Business Hours

Banks are generally open weekdays until 3 or 4; most close by 2 on Friday. Museums are generally open Tuesday through Sunday from 10 to 6 and are closed on Monday; most stop admitting people 30 minutes before closing time. Some have a free-admission day; see individual listings in tours below, but double-check, as the days tend to change. Department stores are open weekdays 10–5 or 6, Saturday until 1. Grocery stores are generally open weekdays from 7 AM to 6 or 7 PM, Saturday until 1 PM; "nonstops," or *éjjel-nappali*, are (theoretically) open 24 hours.

Car Rental

All the major car rental agencies have outlets in Budapest, but rates are high: Daily rates for automatics begin around $55–$60 plus 60¢ per km (½ mi); personal, theft, and accident insurance (not required but recommended) runs an additional $25–$30 per day. Be sure to shop around, as prices can differ greatly. **Avis** and **Hertz** offer Western makes for as much as $550 and more per week. Rates tend to be significantly lower if you arrange your rental from home through the American offices. Smaller local companies, on the other hand, can rent Hungarian cars for as low as $150 per week, although you should watch for hidden insurance conditions. Inquire at **Americana Rent-a-Car** about unlimited mileage weekend specials. Rates include free delivery and pickup of the car anywhere in the city.

➤ MAJOR AGENCIES: **Alamo** (tel. 800/522–9696; 020/8759–6200 in the U.K.). **Avis** (tel. 800/331–1084; 800/331–1084 in Canada; 02/9353–9000 in Australia; 09/525–1982 in New Zealand). **Budget** (tel. 800/527–0700;0870/607–5000 in the U.K., through affiliate Europcar). **Dollar** (tel. 800/800–6000; 0124/622–0111 in the U.K., through affiliate Sixt Kenning; 02/9223–1444 in Australia). **Hertz** (tel. 800/654–3001; 800/263–0600 in Canada; 020/8897–2072 in the U.K.; 02/9669–2444 in Australia; 09/256–8690 in New Zealand) **National Car Rental** (tel. 800/227–7368; 020/8680–4800 in the U.K., where it is known as National Europe).

➤ **Local Agencies: Americana Rent-a-Car** (Ibis Hotel Volga, XIII, Dózsa György út 65, tel. 1/350–2542 or 1/320–8287). **Avis** (main office, V, Szervita tér 8, tel. 1/318–4240; Terminal 2A, tel. 1/296–7265; Terminal 2B, tel. 1/296–6421), **Budget** (main office, Hotel Mercure Buda, I, Krisztina krt. 41–43, tel. 1/214–0420; Terminal 2A, tel. 1/296–8481; Terminal 2B, tel. 1/296–8197), and **Fötaxi** (main office, VII, Kertész u. 24–28, tel. 1/322–1471 or 1/351–0359). **Hertz** (also known in Hungary as Mercure Rent-a-Car; V, Marriott Hotel, Apáczai Csere János u. 4, tel. 1/266–4361; Terminal 2A, tel. 1/296–6988; Terminal 2B, tel. 1/296–7171).

CUTTING COSTS

To get the best deal, **book through a travel agent who will shop around.** Do **look into wholesalers,** companies that do not own fleets but rent in bulk from those that do and often offer better rates than traditional car-rental operations. Payment must be made before you leave home.

➤ **Wholesalers: Auto Europe** (tel. 207/842–2000 or 800/223–5555, fax 800/235–6321, www.autoeurope.com). **DER Travel Services** (9501 W. Devon Ave., Rosemont, IL 60018, tel. 800/782–2424, fax 800/282–7474 for information; 800/860–9944 for brochures, www.dertravel.com). **Kemwel Holiday Autos** (tel. 800/678–0678, fax 914/825–3160, www.kemwel.com).

INSURANCE

When driving a rented car you are generally responsible for any damage to or loss of the vehicle. Before you rent see what coverage your personal auto-insurance policy and credit cards already provide.

Before you buy collision coverage, check your existing policies— you may already be covered. However, collision policies that car-rental companies sell for European rentals usually do not include stolen-vehicle coverage.

REQUIREMENTS & RESTRICTIONS

In Budapest, visitors need an International Driver's Permit; U.S. and Canadian citizens can obtain one from the American or Canadian Automobile Association, respectively. Many car rental agencies will accept an international license, but the formal permit is technically required. A caveat: It can get messy and expensive if you are stopped by a police officer who insists you need an International Driver's License (which, legally, you do). U.K. visitors may use their own domestic licenses. If you intend to drive across a border, **ask about restrictions on driving into other countries.** The minimum age required for renting is usually 21 or older, and some companies also have maximum ages; be sure to inquire when making your arrangements.

A word of caution: If you have any alcohol whatsoever in your body, do not drive. Penalties are fierce, and the blood-alcohol limit is zero.

SURCHARGES

Before you pick up a car in one city and leave it in another, **ask about drop-off charges or one-way service fees,** which can be substantial. Note, too, that some rental agencies charge extra if you return the car before the time specified in your contract. To avoid a hefty refueling fee, **fill the tank just before you turn in the car,** but be aware that gas stations near the rental outlet may overcharge.

Car Travel

Theoretically it's possible to travel by car from the United Kingdom to Hungary, although it's really not recommended due to lack of parts and mechanical know-how. However, if you do choose to drive your own vehicle, don't leave home without the car registration, third-party insurance, driver's license, and (if you're not the car's owner) a notarized letter of permission from the owner. The vehicle must bear a country ID sticker.

AUTO CLUBS

➤ HUNGARY: **Hungarian Automobile Club** (Budapest II, Rómer Flóris u. 4/A, tel. 212–0300).

➤ IN AUSTRALIA: **Australian Automobile Association** (tel. 02/6247–7311).

➤ IN CANADA: **Canadian Automobile Association** (CAA, tel. 613/247–0117).

➤ IN NEW ZEALAND: **New Zealand Automobile Association** (tel. 09/377–4660).

➤ IN THE U.K.: **Automobile Association** (AA, tel. 0990/500–600). **Royal Automobile Club** (RAC, tel. 0990/722–722 for membership; 0345/121–345 for insurance).

➤ IN THE U.S.: **American Automobile Association** (tel. 800/564–6222).

EMERGENCY SERVICES

In case of a breakdown, your best friend is the telephone. Try contacting your **rental agency** or the national breakdown service.

➤ CONTACTS: Hungarian Automobile Club (tel. 188).

GASOLINE

Gas stations are plentiful in Hungary, and many on the main highways stay open all night, even on holidays. Major chains, such as MOL, Shell, and OMV, now have Western-style full-facility stations with rest rooms, brightly lit convenience stores, and 24-hour service. Lines are rarely long, and supplies are essentially stable. Unleaded gasoline (*bleifrei* or *ólommentes*) is generally available at most stations and is usually the 95-octane-level choice. If your car requires unleaded gasoline, be sure to double-check that you're not reaching for the leaded before you pump.

ROAD CONDITIONS

Budapest, like any Western city, is plagued by traffic jams during the day, but motorists should have no problem later in the evening. Parking, however, is a problem—prepare to learn new parking techniques such as curb balancing and sidewalk straddling. Free parking is a thing of the past on most central city streets; hourly fees are paid either to automats or attendants. Motorists not accustomed to sharing the city streets with trams should pay extra attention. You should be prepared to be flagged down numerous times by police conducting routine checks for drunk driving and stolen cars. Be sure all of your papers are in order and readily accessible; unfortunately, the police have been known to give foreigners a hard time.

➤ ROAD MAPS: **Globe Térképbolt** (Globe Map Store; VI, Bajcsy-Zsilinszky út 37, tel. 1/312–6001).

RULES OF THE ROAD

Hungarians drive on the right and observe the usual Continental rules of the road (but they revel in passing). Unless otherwise noted, the speed limit in developed areas is 50 kph (30 mph), on main roads 80–100 kph (50–62 mph), and on highways 120 kph (75 mph). Keep alert: Speed-limit signs are few and far between. Seat belts are compulsory (front-seat belts in lower speed zones, both front and back in higher speed zones), and drinking alcohol is totally prohibited—there is a zero-tolerance policy, and the penalties are very severe.

Children in Budapest

FLYING

If your children are two or older, **ask about children's airfares.** As a general rule, infants under two not occupying a seat fly at greatly reduced fares or even for free. When booking, **confirm carry-on allowances** if you're traveling with infants. In general, for babies charged 10% of the adult fare you are allowed one carry-on bag and a collapsible stroller; if the flight is full, the stroller may have to be checked or you may be limited to less.

Experts agree that it's a good idea to use safety seats aloft for children weighing less than 40 pounds. Airlines set their own policies: U.S. carriers usually require that the child be ticketed, even if he or she is young enough to ride free, since the seats must be strapped into regular seats. Do **check your airline's policy about using safety seats during takeoff and landing.** And since safety seats are not allowed just everywhere in the plane, get your seat assignments early.

When reserving, **request children's meals or a freestanding bassinet** if you need them. But note that bulkhead seats, where you must sit to use the bassinet, may lack an overhead bin or storage space on the floor.

LODGING

Most hotels in Budapest allow children under a certain age to stay in their parents' room at no extra charge, but others charge for them as extra adults; be sure to **find out the cutoff age for children's discounts.** Some spa hotels don't allow children under 12.

The **Novotel** chain which has hotels in Budapest, allows up to two children under 12 to stay free in their parents' room. The **Budapest Hilton** has an unusual policy allowing children of any age—even middle-aged adults—to stay for free in their parents' room.

BEST CHOICES: **Novotel** (tel. 800/221–4542). **Budapest Hilton** (tel. 1/214–3000 in Budapest).

SIGHTS & ATTRACTIONS

Places that are especially appealing to children are indicated by a rubber duckie icon in the margins throughout the book.

SUGGESTED READING

The Adventures of Mickey, Taggy, Pupo, and Cica and How They Discover Budapest, by Kati Rekai (Canadian Stage Arts Publications, Toronto), is an animal fantasy story set in Budapest, written by a Hungarian-born author.

SUPPLIES & EQUIPMENT

In Budapest, disposable diapers and formula are generally available in larger grocery stores and pharmacies. For crayons and craft supplies, try a stationer's.

Customs & Duties

When shopping, **keep receipts** for all purchases. Upon reentering the country, **be ready to show customs officials what you've bought.** If you feel a duty is incorrect or object to the way your clearance was handled, note the inspector's badge number and ask to see a supervisor. If the problem isn't resolved, write to the appropriate authorities, beginning with the port director at your point of entry.

IN HUNGARY

Objects for personal use may be imported freely. If you are over 16, you may bring in 250 cigarettes or 50 cigars or 250 grams of tobacco, plus 2 liters of wine, 1 liter of spirits, and 100 milliliters of perfume. (You also may leave Hungary with this much, plus 5 liters of beer). If you bring in more than 400 dollars in cash and think you may be taking that much out, technically speaking you should declare it on arrival. A customs charge is made on gifts valued in Hungary at more than 30,500 Ft.

If you are bringing any valuables or foreign-made equipment from home, such as cameras, it's wise to carry the original receipts with you or register the items with U.S. Customs before you leave (Form 4457). Otherwise you could end up paying duty upon your return. Be aware that leaving the country without expensive items declared upon entering can present a huge hassle with airport police.

Take care when you leave Hungary that you have the right documentation for exporting goods. Keep receipts of any major purchases. A special permit is needed for works of art, antiques, or objects of museum value. Upon leaving, you are entitled to a value-added tax (VAT) refund on new goods (i.e., not works of art, antiques, or objects of museum value) valued at 50,000 Ft. or more (VAT inclusive). But applying for the refund may rack up more frustration than money: Cash refunds are given only in forints, and you may find yourself in the airport minutes before boarding with a handful of soft currency; while you can take out up to 350,000 forints, converting it back home will be close to impossible. If you otherwise don't have much hard currency on you, you can convert up to about 100,000 of the forints into dollars to come up with the 400-dollars-in-cash export limit. If you made your purchases by credit card you can file for a credit to your card or to your bank account (again in forints), but don't expect it to come through in a hurry. If you intend to apply for the credit, make sure you get customs to stamp the original purchase invoice before you leave the country. For more information, pick up a tax refund brochure from any tourist office or hotel, or contact the **Intel Trade Rt.** in Budapest. For further Hungarian customs information, inquire at the **National Customs and Revenue Office**. If you have trouble communicating, ask **Tourinform** for help.

➤ INFORMATION: **Intel Trade Rt.** (I, Csalogány u. 6-10, tel. 1/201–8120 or 1/356–9800). **National Customs and Revenue Office** (Regional Directorate for Central Hungary, XIV, Hungária krt. 112–114, Budapest, tel. 1/470–4121 or 470–4122). **Tourinform** (tel. 1/317–9800).

IN AUSTRALIA

Australian residents who are 18 or older may bring home $A400 worth of souvenirs and gifts (including jewelry), 250 cigarettes or 250 grams of tobacco, and 1,125 ml of alcohol (including wine, beer, and spirits). Residents under 18 may bring back $A200 worth of goods. Prohibited items include meat products. Seeds, plants, and fruits need to be declared upon arrival.

INFORMATION: **Australian Customs Service** (Regional Director, Box 8, Sydney, NSW 2001, Australia, tel. 02/9213–2000, fax 02/9213–4000, www.customs.gov.au).

IN CANADA

Canadian residents who have been out of Canada for at least 7 days may bring home C$500 worth of goods duty-free. If you've been away less than 7 days but more than 48 hours, the duty-free allowance drops to C$200; if your trip lasts 24–48 hours, the allowance is C$50. You may not pool allowances with family members. Goods claimed under the C$500 exemption may follow you by mail; those claimed under the lesser exemptions must accompany you. Alcohol and tobacco products may be included in the 7-day and 48-hour exemptions but not in the 24-hour exemption. If you meet the age requirements of the province or territory through which you reenter Canada, you may bring in, duty-free, 1.14 liters (40 imperial ounces) of wine or liquor or 24 12-ounce cans or bottles of beer or ale. If you are 16 or older you may bring in, duty-free, 200 cigarettes and 50 cigars. Check ahead of time with Revenue Canada or the Department of Agriculture for policies regarding meat products, seeds, plants, and fruits.

You may send an unlimited number of gifts worth up to C$60 each duty-free to Canada. Label the package UNSOLICITED GIFT—VALUE UNDER $60. Alcohol and tobacco are excluded.

➤ **INFORMATION: Revenue Canada** (2265 St. Laurent Blvd. S, Ottawa, Ontario K1G 4K3, Canada, tel. 613/993–0534; 800/461–9999 in Canada, fax 613/991–4126, www.ccra-adrc.gc.ca).

IN NEW ZEALAND

Homeward-bound residents 17 or older may bring back $700 worth of souvenirs and gifts. Your duty-free allowance also includes 4.5 liters of wine or beer; one 1,125-ml bottle of spirits; and either 200 cigarettes, 250 grams of tobacco, 50 cigars, or a combination of the three up to 250 grams. Prohibited items include meat products, seeds, plants, and fruits.

➤ **INFORMATION: New Zealand Customs** (Custom House, 50 Anzac Ave., Box 29, Auckland, New Zealand, tel. 09/300–5399, fax 09/359–6730), www.customs.govt.nz.

IN THE U.K.

From countries outside the EU, including Eastern and Central Europe, you may bring home, duty-free, 200 cigarettes or 50 cigars; 1 liter of spirits or 2 liters of fortified or sparkling wine or liqueurs; 2 liters of still table wine; 60 ml of perfume; 250 ml of toilet water; plus £136 worth of other goods, including gifts and souvenirs. If returning from outside the EU, prohibited items include meat products, seeds, plants, and fruits.

➤ **INFORMATION: HM Customs and Excise** (Dorset House, Stamford St., Bromley, Kent BR1 1XX, U.K., tel. 020/7202–4227, www.hmce.gov.uk).

IN THE U.S.

U.S. residents who have been out of the country for at least 48 hours (and who have not used the $400 allowance or any part of it in the past 30 days) may bring home $400 worth of foreign goods duty-free.

U.S. residents 21 and older may bring back 1 liter of alcohol duty-free. In addition, regardless of your age, you are allowed 200 cigarettes and 100 non-Cuban cigars. Antiques, which the U.S. Customs Service defines as objects more than 100 years old, enter duty-free, as do original works of art done entirely by hand, including paintings, drawings, and sculptures.

You may also mail or ship packages home duty-free: up to $200 worth of goods for personal use, with a limit of one parcel per addressee per day (except alcohol or tobacco products or perfume worth more than $5); label the package PERSONAL USE and attach a list of its contents and their retail value. Do not label the package UNSOLICITED GIFT or your duty-free exemption will drop to $100. Mailed items do not affect your duty-free allowance on your return.

➤ **INFORMATION: U.S. Customs Service** (1300 Pennsylvania Ave. NW, Washington, DC 20229, www.customs.gov; inquiries tel. 202/354–1000; complaints c/o 1300 Pennsylvania Ave. NW, Room

5.4D, Washington, DC 20229; registration of equipment c/o Resource Management, tel. 202/354–1000).

Dining

(☞ For dining information, *see* Dining *in* Pleasures and Pastimes *in* Introducing Budapest.) The restaurants we list are the cream of the crop in each price category. Unless otherwise noted, the restaurants listed are open daily for lunch and dinner.

RESERVATIONS & DRESS

Reservations are always a good idea: we mention them only when they're essential or not accepted. Book as far ahead as you can, and reconfirm as soon as you arrive. We mention dress only when men are required to wear a jacket or a jacket and tie.

Discounts & Deals

The **Budapest Card** entitles holders to unlimited travel on public transportation; free admission to many museums and sights; and discounts on various services from participating businesses. The cost (at press time) is 2,800 Ft. for two days, 3,400 Ft. for three days; one card is valid for an adult plus one child under 14. It is available at many tourist offices along with a similar pass called the **Hungary Card,** which gives discounts to museums, sights, and service in the entire country.

Be a smart shopper and **compare all your options** before making decisions. A plane ticket bought with a promotional coupon from travel clubs, coupon books, and direct-mail offers may not be cheaper than the least expensive fare from a discount ticket agency. And always keep in mind that what you get is just as important as what you save.

DISCOUNT RESERVATIONS

To save money, **look into discount reservations services** with toll-free numbers, which use their buying power to get a better price on hotels, airline tickets, even car rentals. When booking a room, always **call the hotel's local toll-free number** (if one is available) rather than the central reservations number—you'll often get a better price. Always ask about special packages or corporate rates.

When shopping for the best deal on hotels and car rentals, **look for guaranteed exchange rates,** which protect you against a falling dollar. With your rate locked in, you won't pay more, even if the price goes up in the local currency.

➤ AIRLINE TICKETS: tel. 800/FLY–ASAP.

➤ HOTEL ROOMS: **International Marketing & Travel Concepts** (tel. 800/790–4682). **Steigenberger Reservation Service** (tel. 800/223–5652, www.srs-worldhotels.com). **Travel Interlink** (tel. 800/888–5898, www.travelinterlink.com).

Electricity

To use your U.S.-purchased electric-powered equipment, **bring a converter and adapter.** The electrical current in Eastern and Central Europe is 220 volts, 50 cycles alternating current (AC); wall outlets generally take plugs with two round prongs.

If your appliances are dual-voltage, you'll need only an adapter. Don't use 110-volt outlets marked FOR SHAVERS ONLY for high-wattage appliances such as blow-dryers. Most laptops operate equally well on 110 and 220 volts and so require only an adapter.

Embassies

Australian Embassy (XII, Királyhágó tér 8–9, tel. 1/201–8899). **Canadian Embassy** (XII, Zugligeti út 51–53, tel. 1/275–1200). **British Embassy** (V, Harmincad u. 6, tel. 1/266–2888, fax 1/266–0907). **U.S. Embassy** (V, Szabadság tér 12, tel. 1/475–4400). There are no New Zealand embassies or consulates in Budapest.

Emergencies

For a 24-hour private ambulance service with English-speaking personnel, call **Falck–SOS.** If you need to see a doctor, ask your hotel or embassy for recommendations, or visit the **R-Clinic,** a private clinic staffed by English-speaking doctors offering 24-hour medical and ambulance service. The clinic accepts major credit cards and prepares full reports for your insurance company. U.S. and Canadian visitors are advised to take out full medical insurance. U.K. visitors are covered for emergencies and essential treatment. **Professional Dental Associates** is a private, English-speaking dental practice consisting of Western-trained dentists and hygienists; service is available 24 hours a day.

Most pharmacies close between 6 PM and 8 PM, but several pharmacies stay open at night and on the weekend, offering 24-hour service, with a small surcharge for items that aren't officially stamped as urgent by a physician. You must ring the buzzer next to the night window and someone will respond over the intercom. Staff is unlikely to speak English; ask for help from someone who speaks Hungarian. Central ones in Pest include those at **Teréz körút 41** in the sixth district, near the Nyugati train station; and the one at **Rákóczi út 39** in the 8th district, near the Keleti train station. In Buda, there is one across the street from the Déli train station at **Alkotás utca 1/b** in the 12th district.

➤ DOCTORS & DENTISTS: **Doctor: R-Clinic** (II, Felsőzöldmáli út 13, tel. 1/325–9999) **Dentist: Professional Dental Associates** (II, Sodrás u. 9, tel. 1/200–4447 or 1/200–4448).

➤ EMERGENCY SERVICES: **Ambulance** (tel. 104), **Falck–SOS** (II, Kapy u. 49/b, tel. 1/200–0100), a 24-hour private ambulance service with English-speaking personnel. **Police** (tel. 107).

➤ 24-HOUR PHARMACIES: **Teréz körút 41** (tel. 1/311–4439), **Rákóczi út 39** (tel. 1/314–3695), **Alkotás utca 1/b** (tel. 1/355–4691).

Health

You may gain weight, but there are few other serious health hazards for the traveler in Budapest. Tap water may taste bad but is generally drinkable (though see the precautions below); when it runs rusty out of the tap or the aroma of chlorine is overpowering, it might help to have some iodine tablets or bottled water handy.

Vegetarians and those on special diets may have a problem with the heavy local cuisine, which is based largely on pork and beef. To prevent your vitamin intake from dropping to danger levels, buy fresh fruits and vegetables at seasonal street markets— regular grocery stores often don't sell them.

To avoid problems clearing customs, diabetic travelers carrying needles and syringes should have on hand a letter from their physician confirming their need for insulin injections. No vaccinations are required for entry into Budapest.

OVER-THE-COUNTER REMEDIES

Pharmacies throughout Budapest carry a variety of nonprescription as well as prescription drugs. For recommended pharmacies, *see* Emergencies, above.

Holidays

January 1; March 15 (Anniversary of 1848 Revolution); April 15–16, 2001 and March 31–April 1, 2002 (Easter and Easter Monday); May 1 (Labor Day); June 3–4, 2001 and May 19–20, 2002 (Pentecost); August 20 (St. Stephen's and Constitution Day); October 23 (1956 Revolution Day); December 24–26.

Insurance

The most useful travel-insurance plan is a comprehensive policy that includes coverage for trip cancellation and interruption, default, trip delay, and medical expenses (with a waiver for pre-existing conditions).

Without insurance you will lose all or most of your money if you cancel your trip, regardless of the reason. Default insurance covers you if your tour operator, airline, or cruise line goes out of business. Trip-delay covers expenses that arise because of bad weather or mechanical delays. Study the fine print when comparing policies.

When you're traveling internationally, a key component of travel insurance is coverage for medical bills incurred if you get sick on the road. Such expenses are not generally covered by Medicare or private policies. U.K. residents can buy a travel-insurance policy valid for most vacations taken during the year in which it's purchased (but check pre-existing-condition coverage). British and Australian citizens need extra medical coverage when traveling overseas.

Always **buy travel policies directly from the insurance company**; if you buy them from a cruise line, airline, or tour operator that goes out of business you probably will not be covered for the agency or operator's default, a major risk. Before making any purchase, **review your existing health and home-owner's policies** to find what they cover away from home.

➤ TRAVEL INSURERS: In the U.S.: **Access America** (6600 W. Broad St., Richmond, VA 23230, tel. 804/285–3300 or 800/284–8300, fax 804/673–1586, www.previewtravel.com), **Travel Guard International** (1145 Clark St., Stevens Point, WI 54481, tel. 715/345–0505 or 800/826–1300, fax 800/955–8785, www.noelgroup.com).

➤ INSURANCE INFORMATION: In the U.K.: **Association of British Insurers** (51–55 Gresham St., London EC2V 7HQ, U.K., tel. 020/7600–3333, fax 020/7696–8999, www.abi.org.uk). In Canada: **Voyager Insurance** (44 Peel Center Dr., Brampton, Ontario L6T 4M8, Canada, tel. 905/791–8700, 800/668–4342 in Canada). In Australia: **Insurance Council of Australia** (tel. 03/9614–1077, fax 03/9614–7924). In New Zealand: **Insurance Council of New Zealand** (Box 474, Wellington, New Zealand, tel. 04/472–5230, fax 04/473–3011, www.icnz.org.nz).

Language

Hungarian (*Magyar*) tends to look and sound intimidating at first because it is not an Indo-European language. Generally, older people speak some German, and many younger people speak at least rudimentary English, which has become the most popular language to learn. It's a safe bet that anyone in the tourist trade will speak at least one of the two languages. Also note that when giving names, Hungarians put the family name before the given name.

Lodging

Reservations are vital if you plan to visit Budapest during the summer season. Reservations are a good idea but aren't imperative if you decide to strike out into the countryside. For more information, *see* Lodging in Pleasures and Pastimes in Introducing Budapest. The lodgings we list are the cream of the crop in each price category. We always list the facilities that are available—but we don't specify whether they cost extra: when pricing accommodations, always ask what's included and what costs extra.

APARTMENT RENTALS

Apartments, available for short- and long-term rental, can be the most economic lodging for families or groups. A short-term rental in Budapest may cost anywhere from $30 to $60 a day. The best bet is to go through an agency.

Amadeus Apartments oversees five well-kept apartments in downtown Budapest, each consisting of two rooms plus a fully equipped kitchen and bathroom. Free transportation from the train station or airport is included; guarded parking areas are provided for a fee for those with cars. The two-person, high-season rate is approximately $40 a night. **TRIBUS Welcome Hotel Service**, open 24 hours a day, books private apartments, arranges rooms in private homes, and reserves rooms in inns and hotels. **Cooptourist** arranges private apartments and rooms and makes reservations in its affiliated inns and hotels.

➤ INTERNATIONAL AGENTS: **Hometours International** (Box 11503, Knoxville, TN 37939, tel. 865/690–8484 or 800/367–4668, http://thor.he.net/~hometour/). **Interhome** (1990 N.E. 163rd St.,

Suite 110, N. Miami Beach, FL 33162, tel. 305/940–2299 or 800/ 882–6864, fax 305/940–2911, www.interhome.com).

➤ LOCAL AGENTS: **Amadeus Apartments** (IX, Üllői út 197, H-1091, tel. 06/309–422–893); **TRIBUS Welcome Hotel Service** (V, Apáczai Csere János u. 1, tel. 1/318–5776); **Cooptourist** (XI, Bartók Béla út 4, tel. 1/466–5349).

B&BS

Although B&Bs of the traditional English variety aren't prevalent in Budapest, there are numerous variations on the concept available, including comfortable and elaborately decorated facilities.The rate per night for a double room is around $20 (which usually includes the use of a bathroom but not breakfast).

➤ B&B RESERVATION SERVICES: **TRIBUS Hotel Service** (☞ *above*) and **Cooptourist** (☞ *above*).

HOSTELS

No matter what your age you can **save on lodging costs by staying at hostels.** In some 5,000 locations in more than 70 countries around the world, Hostelling International (HI), the umbrella group for a number of national youth-hostel associations, offers single-sex, dorm-style beds and, at many hostels, couples rooms and family accommodations. Membership in any HI national hostel association, open to travelers of all ages, allows you to stay in HI-affiliated hostels at member rates (one-year membership is about $25 for adults; hostels run about $10–$25 per night). Members also have priority if the hostel is full; they're eligible for discounts around the world, even on rail and bus travel in some countries.

In Budapest, most hostels are geared toward the college crowd. Among several good ones are the friendly, Internet-equipped **Back Pack Guesthouse,** where rates range from 1,300 Ft. (8-10 bed rooms) to 1,900 Ft. (2-bed rooms), and the **Sirály Youth Hostel**, situated in the relative peace, quiet, and clean air of an island-park on the Danube, where the per-person rate in 12-bed rooms is 1,400 Ft. For further information, consult the free annual accommodations directory published by **Tourinform** (☞ Visitor Information, below) or the listings in **Budapest In Your Pocket**, available at newsstands.

➤ **Information: Back Pack Guesthouse** (XI, Takács Menyhért u. 33, tel. 1/385–8946) **Sirály Youth Hostel** (XIII, Margit-sziget (Margaret Island), tel. 1/329–3952).

➤ **Organizations: Hostelling International—American Youth Hostels** (733 15th St. NW, Suite 840, Washington, DC 20005, tel. 202/783–6161, fax 202/783–6171, www.hiayh.org). **Hostelling International—Canada** (400–205 Catherine St., Ottawa, Ontario K2P 1C3, Canada, tel. 613/237–7884, fax 613/237–7868, www.hostellingintl.ca). **Youth Hostel Association of England and Wales** (Trevelyan House, 8 St. Stephen's Hill, St. Albans, Hertfordshire AL1 2DY, U.K., tel. 0870/8708808, fax 01727/844126, www.yha.org.uk). **Australian Youth Hostel Association** (10 Mallett St., Camperdown, NSW 2050, Australia, tel. 02/9565–1699, fax 02/9565–1325, www.yha.com.au). **Youth Hostels Association of New Zealand** (Box 436, Christchurch, New Zealand, tel. 03/379–9970, fax 03/365–4476, www.yha.org.nz).

HOTELS

Throughout the past decade the quality of hotels in Budapest improved notably. Many formerly state-run hotels were privatized, much to their benefit—a transition process that is still on-going in some countries. International hotel chains have established a strong presence in the city; while they may not be strong on local character, they do provide a reliably high standard of quality.

Hotels listed throughout the book have private bath unless otherwise noted.

➤ **Toll-Free Numbers: Best Western** (tel. 800/528–1234, www.bestwestern.com). **Choice** (tel. 800/221–2222, www.

hotelchoice.com). **Hilton** (tel. 800/445–8667, www.hilton.com). **Holiday Inn** (tel. 800/465–4329, www.basshotels.com). **Hungarian Hotels** (tel. 800/448–4321). **Hyatt Hotels & Resorts** (tel. 800/233–1234, www.hyatt.com). **Inter-Continental** (tel. 800/327–0200, www.interconti.com). **Marriott** (tel. 800/228–9290, www.marriott.com).

Mail & Shipping

Airmail letters and postcards generally take seven days to travel between Hungary and the United States. They can take more than twice as long during the Christmas season.

The main post office branch is in downtown Budapest. The post office near the Keleti (East) train station stays open until 9 PM all week, and the branch near the Nyugati (west) train station is open until 9 PM on weekdays but shuts its doors at 8 PM on weekends. The American Express office also has poste restante services.

➤ POST OFFICES: **American Express** Deák Ferenc u. 10 H-1052 Budapest, tel. 1/235–4330. **Downtown post office** Magyar Posta 4. sz., Városház u. 18, H-1052 Budapest. **Keleti branch** (VIII, Baross tér) **Nyugati branch** (VI, Teréz krt. 51).

POSTAL RATES

Postage for an airmail letter to the United States costs about 160 Ft.; an airmail letter to the United Kingdom and elsewhere in Western Europe costs about 150 Ft. Airmail postcards to the United States cost about 110 Ft. and to the United Kingdom and the rest of Western Europe, about 100 Ft.

Metro Travel

Service on Budapest's subways is cheap, fast, frequent, and comfortable; stations are easily located on maps and streets by the big letter M (for metro). Tickets—95 Ft.; valid on all forms of mass transportation—can be bought at hotels, metro stations, newsstands, and kiosks. They are valid for one ride only; you can't change lines or direction. Tickets must be canceled in the time-clock machines in station entrances and should be kept until the end of the journey, as there are frequent checks by undercover inspectors; a fine for traveling without a validated ticket is about 1,300 Ft. A *napijegy* (day ticket) costs 740 Ft. (a three-day "tourist ticket," 1,500 Ft.) and allows unlimited travel on all services within the city limits.

Line 1 (marked FÖLDALATTI), which starts downtown at Vörösmarty tér and follows Andrássy út out past Gundel restaurant and City Park, is an antique tourist attraction in itself, built in the 1890s for the Magyar Millennium; its yellow trains with tank treads still work. Lines 2 and 3 were built 90 years later. Line 2 (red) runs from the eastern suburbs, past the Keleti (East) Station, through the city center, and under the Danube to the Déli (South) Station. (One of the stations, Moszkva tér, is where the *Várbusz* [Castle Bus] can be boarded.) Line 3 (blue) runs from the southeastern suburbs to Deák tér, through the city center, and northward to the Nyugati (West) Station and the northern suburbs. On all three lines, fare tickets are canceled in machines at the station entrance. All three metro lines meet at the Deák tér station and run from 4:30 AM to shortly after 11 PM.

Money Matters

COSTS

Cup of coffee, 120 Ft.–200 Ft.; bottle of beer, 350 Ft.–550 Ft.; soft drinks, 150 Ft.; ham sandwich, 200 Ft.; 2-km (1-mi) taxi ride, 300 Ft.; museum admission, 150 Ft.–300 Ft. Prices throughout this guide are given for adults. Substantially reduced fees are almost always available for children, students, and senior citizens. For information on taxes, *see* Taxes, *below*.

ATMS

Twenty-four-hour cash machines have sprung up throughout Budapest; some accept Plus network bank cards and Visa credit cards, others Cirrus and MasterCard. You can withdraw forints only (automatically converted at the bank's official exchange rate) directly from your account. Most levy a 1% or $3 service charge. Instructions are in English.

CREDIT CARDS

Plastic has recently entered Budapest's financial scene: Most major credit cards are accepted in hotels, restaurants, and shops that cater regularly to foreign tourists and business travelers, though don't rely on them in less expensive accommodations and restaurants. When you leave the beaten path, be prepared to pay cash. Always inquire about credit card policies when booking hotel rooms. Visa and EuroCard/ MasterCard are the most commonly accepted credit cards in Budapest.

It's smart to **write down (and keep separate) the number of each credit card you're carrying** along with the international service phone number that usually appears on the back of the card.

Throughout this guide, the following abbreviations are used: **AE,** American Express; **D,** Discover; **DC,** Diners Club; **MC,** Master Card; and **V,** Visa.

CURRENCY

Hungary's unit of currency is the forint (Ft.), no longer divided into fillérs as it was a few years ago. There are bills of 200, 500, 1,000, 2,000, 5,000, and 10,000 forints (at press time one of 20,000 forints was also planned); and coins of 1, 2, 5, 10, 20, 50, and 100 forints. The exchange rate was approximately 302 Ft. to the U.S. dollar, 204 Ft. to the Canadian dollar, and 427 Ft. to the pound sterling at press time.

The forint was significantly devalued over the last few years and continues its decline, but at press time inflation had fallen under 10% from the 25% of five years ago. You'll receive more forints for your dollar but will find that prices have risen to keep up with inflation. More and more hotels now set their rates in hard currency to avoid the forint's instability. Still, even with inflation and the 25% value-added tax (VAT) in the service industry, enjoyable vacations with all the trimmings still remain less expensive than in nearby Western cities such as Vienna.

CURRENCY EXCHANGE

There is still a black market in hard currency, but changing money on the street is risky and illegal, and the bank rate almost always comes close. Stick with banks and official exchange offices.

For the most favorable rates, **change money through banks.** Although ATM transaction fees may be higher abroad than at home, ATM rates are excellent because they are based on wholesale rates offered only by major banks. You won't do as well at exchange booths in airports or rail and bus stations, in hotels, in restaurants, or in stores, although you may find their hours more convenient. To avoid lines at airport exchange booths, **get a bit of local currency before you leave home.** For those without plastic, many cash-exchange machines, into which you feed paper currency for forints, have also sprung up. Most bank automats and cash-exchange machines are clustered around their respective bank branches throughout downtown Pest.

EXCHANGE SERVICES: **International Currency Express** (tel. 888/278–6628 for orders, www.foreignmoney.com). **Thomas Cook Currency Services** (tel. 800/287–7362 for telephone orders and retail locations, www.us.thomascook.com).

TRAVELER'S CHECKS

Eurocheque holders can cash personal checks in all banks and in most hotels. Many banks now also cash American Express and Visa traveler's checks. **American Express** has a full-service office in Budapest which also dispenses cash to its cardholders; a smaller branch on Castle Hill—at the Sisi Restaurant —has a currency exchange which operates daily from March to mid-

January. Budapest also has a **Citibank** offering full services to account holders, including a 24-hour cash machine.

➤ INFORMATION: **American Express**(V, Deák Ferenc u. 10, tel. 1/235–4330, fax 1/267–2028), Castle Hill branch: (tel. 1/264–0118) **Citibank** (V, Vörösmarty tér 4).

Passports & Visas

When traveling internationally, **carry your passport** even if you don't need one (it's always the best form of I.D.) and **make two photocopies of the data page** (one for someone at home and another for you, carried separately from your passport). If you lose your passport, promptly call the nearest embassy or consulate and the local police.

ENTERING BUDAPEST

Only a valid passport is required of U.S., British, and Canadian citizens; Australian citizens need a visa. For additional information contact the **Hungarian Embassy.**

HUNGARIAN EMBASSIES: United States: (3910 Shoemaker St. NW, Washington, DC 20008, tel. 202/362–6730), Canada: (299 Waverley St. Ottawa, Ontario K2P 0V9, tel. 613/230–9614), London: (35b Eaton Pl., London SW1X 8BY, tel. 0171/235–5218), Australia: (17 Beale Crescent Deakin Act., Canberra 2600, tel. 6126/282–3226).

PASSPORT OFFICES

The best time to apply for a passport or to renew is in fall and winter. Before any trip, check your passport's expiration date, and, if necessary, renew it as soon as possible.

Rest Rooms

While the rest rooms at Budapest's Ferihegy Airport may sparkle and smell of soap, don't expect the same of those at the train and bus stations—which, by the way, usually have attendants on hand who collect a fee of about 40 Ft. Pay the attendant on the way in; you will receive toilet tissue in exchange. Since public rest rooms are generally few and far between, you will sometimes find yourself entering cafés, bars, or restaurants primarily to use their toilets; when doing so, unless it happens to be a bustling fast-food place, you should probably order a little something.

Safety

Crime rates are still relatively low in Budapest, but travelers should beware of pickpockets in crowded areas, especially on public transportation, at railway stations, and in big hotels. In general, always keep your valuables with you—in open bars and restaurants, purses hung on or placed next to chairs are easy targets. Make sure your wallet is safe in a buttoned pocket, or watch your handbag.

Car theft is also a concern. While a typical rental car is less likely to be stolen, expensive German makes such as Audi, BMW, and Mercedes are hot targets for car thieves.

WOMEN IN BUDAPEST

Women generally move about Budapest with no more problems than they'd encounter in any western European city. The same general precautions apply: It isn't wise for a woman to go alone to a bar or nightclub or to wander the streets late at night. When traveling by train at night, seek out compartments that are well populated.

Sightseeing Tours

BOAT TOURS

From late March through October boats leave from the dock at Vigadó tér on 1½-hour cruises between the railroad bridges north and south of the Árpád and Petőfi bridges, respectively. The trip, organized by **MAHART Tours**, runs only on weekends and holidays (once a day, at noon) in April and May, then twice daily from May to October (at noon and 7); the cost is about 900

Ft. From mid-June through August, the evening cruise leaves at 7:45 and has live music and dancing for 100 Ft. more.

Hour-long evening sightseeing cruises on the **Danube Legend** depart nightly at 8:15 in April and October, and three times nightly (at 8:15, 9, and 10) from May through September. Guests receive headphones and listen to a recorded explanation of the sights in the language of their choice. Drinks are also served. Boats depart from Pier 6–7 at Vigadó tér (tel. 1/317–2203 for reservations and information).

The **Duna-Bella** takes guests on two-hour tours on the Danube, including a one-hour walk on Margaret Island and shipboard cocktails. Recorded commentary is provided through earphones. The tour is offered July through August, six times a day; May through June and in September, three times a day; and April and October, once a day. Boats depart from Pier 6–7 at Vigadó tér (tel. 1/317–2203 for reservations and information).

FEES & SCHEDULES: Danube Legend (tel. 1/317–2203), **Duna-Bella** (tel. 1/317–2203), **MAHART Tours** (tel. 1/318–1223).

BUS TOURS

IBUSZ Travel conducts three-hour bus tours of the city that operate all year and cost about 5,500 Ft. Starting from Erzsébet tér, they take in parts of both Buda and Pest.

Cityrama also offers a three-hour city bus tour (about 5,500 Ft. per person). Both have commentary in English.

IBUSZ, Cityrama, and **Budapest Tourist** organize a number of unusual tours, with trips to the Buda Hills, goulash parties, and visits to such traditional sites as the National Gallery and Parliament. These companies will provide English-speaking personal guides on request. Also check at your hotel.

Jewish-Heritage Tours: Chosen Tours offers a three-hour combination bus and walking tour ($17) called "Budapest Through Jewish Eyes," highlighting the sights and cultural life of the city's Jewish history. Tours run daily except Saturday and include free pickup and drop-off at central locations. Arrangements can also be made for off-season tours, as well as custom-designed tours.

Fees & Schedules: Budapest Tourist (I, Déli pályaudvar [South Railway Station]), tel. 1/212–4625 or 1/355–7167. **Chosen Tours** (XII, Pagony u. 40, tel./fax 1/355–2202). **Cityrama** (V, Báthori u. 22, tel. 1/302–4382). **IBUSZ Travel** (V, Ferenciek tere 10, tel. 1/485–2762 or 1/317–7767).

PRIVATE GUIDES

The major travel agencies—**IBUSZ Travel** and **Budapest Tourist** (☞ Fees & Schedules, *above*)—will arrange for guides.

Taxes

VALUE-ADDED TAX

Global Refund is a VAT refund service that makes getting your money back hassle-free. The service is available Europe-wide at 130,000 affiliated stores. In participating stores, **ask for the Global Refund refund form** (called a Shopping Cheque). Have it stamped like any customs form by customs officials when you leave the European Union (be ready to show customs officials what you've bought). Then take the form to one of the more than 700 Global Refund counters—conveniently located at every major airport and border crossing—and your money will be refunded on the spot in the form of cash, check, or a refund to your credit-card account (minus a small percentage for processing).

VAT Refunds: Global Refund (707 Summer St., Stamford, CT 06901, tel. 800/566–9828, fax 203/674–8709, www.globalrefund.com).

Taxis

Taxis are plentiful and a good value, but make sure they have a working meter. The average initial charge is 125 Ft.–200 Ft. (toward the latter between 10 PM and 6 AM), plus about the same per km (½ mi) and 50 Ft.–70 Ft. (again, more at night) per minute of waiting time. Many drivers try to charge outrageous prices, especially if they sense that their passenger is a tourist. Avoid unmarked, "freelance" taxis; stick with those affiliated with an established company. Your safest and most reliable bet is to do what the locals do: Order a taxi by phone; it will arrive in about 5–10 minutes. The best rates are with **BudaTaxi** (tel. 1/233–3333)), **Citytaxi** (tel. 1/211–1111), **Fő taxi** (tel. 1/222–2222), **Tele 5 Taxi** (tel. 1/355–5555), and **6x6 Taxi** (tel. 1/266–6666).

Telephones

Though continuously improving, the Hungarian telephone system is still antiquated, especially in the countryside. Be patient. With the slow improvements comes the problem of numbers changing—sometimes without forewarning. Tens of thousands of phone numbers in Budapest alone will be changed over the next few years; if you're having trouble getting through, ask your concierge to check the number for you.

AREA & COUNTRY CODES

The country code for Hungary is 36. When dialing from outside the country, drop the initial 06 prefix for area codes outside of Budapest. The country code for the United States is 1 for the United States and Canada, 61 for Australia, 64 for New Zealand, and 44 for the U.K.

DIRECTORY & OPERATOR ASSISTANCE

Dial 198 for directory assistance for all of Hungary. Operators are unlikely to speak English. A safer bet is to consult *The Phone Book*, an English-language telephone directory full of important Budapest numbers as well as cultural and tourist information; it's provided in guest rooms of most major hotels, as well as at many restaurants and English-language bookstores. A similar, though much slimmer guide is *Budapest in Your Pocket*, which appears five times a year and can be found at newsstands and hotels.

INTERNATIONAL CALLS

Direct calls to foreign countries can be made from Budapest and all major provincial towns by dialing oo and waiting for the international dialing tone; on pay phones the initial charge is 60 Ft. To reach an **AT&T** long-distance operator, dial tel. 06–800–01111; for **MCI**, dial tel. 06–800–01411; for **Sprint,** dial tel. 06–800–01877.

LOCAL CALLS

The city code for Budapest is 1; it is unnecessary to use this code when calling within the city.

LONG-DISTANCE CALLS

Within Hungary, most towns can be dialed directly—dial 06 and wait for the buzzing tone; then dial the local number. Note that cellular phone numbers are treated like long-distance domestic calls: Dial 06 before the number (when giving their cellular phone numbers, most people include the 06 anyway).

LONG-DISTANCE SERVICES

AT&T, MCI, and Sprint access codes make calling long distance relatively convenient, but you may find the local access number blocked in many hotel rooms. First ask the hotel operator to connect you. If the hotel operator balks, ask for an international operator, or dial the international operator yourself. One way to improve your odds of getting connected to your long-distance carrier is to travel with more than one company's calling card (a hotel may block Sprint, for example, but not MCI). If all else fails, call from a pay phone.

➤ Access Codes: AT&T Direct (tel. 0080001111). MCI WorldPhone (tel. 0680001411). Sprint International Access (tel. 0680001877).

PUBLIC PHONES

Coin-operated pay phones accept 10-Ft., 20-Ft., 50-Ft., and 100-Ft. coins; the minimum initial amount is 20 Ft. Given that they often swallow up change without allowing a call in exchange, however, when possible use gray card-operated telephones, which outnumber coin-operated phones in Budapest. The cards—available at post offices and most newsstands and kiosks—come in units of 60 (800 Ft.) and 90 (1,800 Ft.) calls. Don't be surprised if a flock of children gathers around your pay phone while you talk—collecting and trading used phone cards is a raging fad.

Time

Budapest is on Central European Time (CET), one hour ahead of Greenwich Mean Time and six hours ahead of the eastern time zone of the United States.

Tipping

Four decades of socialism have not restrained the extended palm in Budapest—so tip when in doubt. Hairdressers and taxi drivers expect 10%–15% tips, while porters should get a dollar or two. Coatroom attendants receive 100 Ft.–200 Ft., as do gas-pump attendants if they wash your windows or check your tires; dressing-room attendants at thermal baths receive 50 Ft.–100 Ft. for opening and closing your locker. Gratuities are not included automatically on bills at most restaurants; when the waiter arrives with the bill, you should immediately add a 10%–15% tip to the amount, as it is not customary to leave the tip on the table. If a Gypsy band plays exclusively for your table, you should leave at least 200 Ft. in a plate discreetly provided for that purpose.

Tours & Packages

Because everything is prearranged on a prepackaged tour or independent vacation, you'll spend less time planning—and often get it all at a good price.

BOOKING WITH AN AGENT

Travel agents are excellent resources. But it's a good idea to collect brochures from several agencies as some agents' suggestions may be influenced by relationships with tour and package firms that reward them for volume sales. If you have a special interest, **find an agent with expertise in that area**; the American Society of Travel Agents (ASTA; ☞ Travel Agencies, *below*) has a database of specialists worldwide.

Make sure your travel agent knows the accommodations and other services of the place they're recommending. Ask about the hotel's location, room size, beds, and whether it has a pool, room service, or programs for children, if you care about these. Has your agent been there in person or sent others whom you can contact?

Do some homework on your own, too: local tourism boards can provide information about lesser-known and small-niche operators, some of which may sell only direct.

BUYER BEWARE

Each year consumers are stranded or lose their money when tour operators—even large ones with excellent reputations—go out of business. So **check out the operator.** Ask several travel agents about its reputation, and try to **book with a company that has a consumer-protection program.** (Look for information in the company's brochure.) In the United States, members of the National Tour Association and the United States Tour Operators Association are required to set aside funds to cover your payments and travel arrangements in the event that the company defaults. It's also a good idea to choose a company that participates in the American Society of Travel Agents' Tour Operator Program (TOP); ASTA will act as mediator in any disputes between you and your tour operator.

Remember that the more your package or tour includes the better you can predict the ultimate cost of your vacation. Make sure you know exactly what is covered, and **beware of hidden costs.** Are taxes, tips, and transfers included? Entertainment and excursions? These can add up.

➤ TOUR-OPERATOR RECOMMENDATIONS: **American Society of Travel Agents** (☞ Travel Agencies, *below*). **National Tour Association**

(NTA; 546 E. Main St., Lexington, KY 40508, tel. 859/226–4444 or 800/682–8886, www.ntaonline.com). **United States Tour Operators Association** (USTOA; 342 Madison Ave., Suite 1522, New York, NY 10173, tel. 212/599–6599 or 800/468–7862, fax 212/599–6744, www.ustoa.com).

Train Travel to and from Budapest

Although trains in Budapest can mean hours of sitting on a hard seat in a smoky car, traveling by rail is very inexpensive. Rail networks in Hungary are very extensive, though trains can be infuriatingly slow and it is rare to find one running less than full or almost so. You'll invariably enjoy interesting and friendly traveling company, however; most Hungarians are eager to hear about the West and to discuss the enormous changes in their own countries.

There are three main *pályaudvar* (train stations) in Budapest: **Déli** (South) station, **Keleti** (East) which receives most international rail traffic coming in from the west, and **Nyugati** (West) which handles a combination of international and domestic trains. Call the 24-hour phone numbers for information on trains in and out of any station. Trains to and from Vienna usually operate from the Keleti Station, while those to the Lake Balaton region depart from the Déli. There are no direct trains from London. Sofia has service to Budapest, but for travelers without the necessary visas, it can be a long, out-of-the-way journey to skirt Serbia.

Travel by train from Budapest to other large cities is cheap and efficient. Remember to take **Intercity (IC)** trains—which are especially clean and fast, but require a *helyjegy* (seat reservation) for about 350 Ft.—or *gyorsvonat* (express trains) and not *személyvonat* (locals), which are extremely slow. On timetables, tracks (*vágány*) are abbreviated with a "v;" *indul* means departing, while *érkezik* means arriving. Trains get crowded during weekend travel in summer; you're more likely to have elbow room if you pay a little extra for first-class tickets.

➤ **Train Information: Keleti** (East; VIII, Baross tér); **Nyugati** (West; V, Nyugati tér), and **Déli** (South; XII, Alkotás u.). 24-hour information: International trains: tel. 1/461–5500; Domestic trains: tel. 1/461–5400.

CUTTING COSTS

To save money, **look into rail passes.** But be aware that if you don't plan to cover many miles you may come out ahead by buying individual tickets.

Only Hungarian citizens are entitled to student discounts on train fares; all senior citizens (men over 60, women over 55), however, are eligible for a 20% discount. InterRail cards are available for those under 26, and the Rail Europe Senior Travel Pass entitles senior citizens to a 30% reduction on all train fares. Snacks and drinks are becoming less available on trains, so pack a lunch for the road; train picnics are a way of life. For more information about rail travel, contact or visit **MAV Passenger Service.**

There are several passes valid in Hungary. You can use the **European East Pass** on the national rail networks of Hungary, Austria, the Czech Republic, Poland, and Slovakia. The pass covers five days of unlimited first-class travel within a one-month period for $205. Additional travel days may be purchased. You can also combine the East Pass with a national rail pass. The **Hungarian Flexipass** costs $64 for five days of unlimited first-class train travel within a 15-day period or $80 for 10 days within a one-month period.

Hungary is also the rare Eastern European country that is covered by a **Eurailpass,** which provides unlimited first-class rail travel, in all of the participating countries, for the duration of the pass. These are available for 15 days ($554), 21 days ($718), one month ($890), two months ($1,260), and three months ($1,558). For further information, *see* Train Travel to and from Budapest, *above.*

Many travelers assume that rail passes guarantee them seats on the trains they wish to ride. Not so. You need to **book seats ahead even if you are using a rail pass**; seat reservations are required on some European trains, particularly high-speed trains, and are a good idea on trains that may be crowded—particularly in summer on popular routes. You will also need a reservation if you purchase sleeping accommodations.

INFORMATION AND PASSES: Rail Europe (500 Mamaroneck Ave., Harrison, NY 10528, tel. 914/682–5172 or 800/438–7245, fax 800/432–1329; 2087 Dundas E, Suite 106, Mississauga, Ontario L4X 1M2, tel. 800/361–7245, fax 905/602–4198). **DER Travel Services** (9501 W. Devon Ave., Rosemont, IL 60018, tel. 800/782–2424, fax 800/282–7474 for information; 800/860–9944 for brochures). **CIT Tours Corp.** (15 West 44th Street, 10th Floor, New York, NY 10036, tel. 212/730–2400; 800/248–7245 in the U.S.; 800/387–0711; 800/361–7799 in Canada). **MAV Passenger Service** (VI, Andrássy út 35, Budapest, tel. 1/461–5500 international information; 1/461–5400 domestic information).

Travel Agencies

A good travel agent puts your needs first. Look for an agency that has been in business at least five years, emphasizes customer service, and has someone on staff who specializes in your destination. In addition, **make sure the agency belongs to a professional trade organization.** The American Society of Travel Agents (ASTA), with 27,000 agents in some 170 countries, is the largest and most influential in the field. Operating under the motto "Integrity in Travel," it maintains and enforces a strict code of ethics and will step in to help mediate any agent-client disputes if necessary. ASTA also maintains a Web site that includes a directory of agents. (If a travel agency is also acting as your tour operator, *see* Buyer Beware in Tours & Packages, *above*.)

➤ **LOCAL AGENT REFERRALS: American Society of Travel Agents** (ASTA; tel. 800/965–2782 24-hr hot line, fax 703/684–8319, www.astanet.com). **Association of British Travel Agents** (68–71 Newman St., London W1P 4AH, U.K., tel. 020/7637–2444, fax 020/7637–0713, www.abtanet.com). **Association of Canadian Travel Agents** (1729 Bank St., Suite 201, Ottawa, Ontario K1V 7Z5,

Canada, tel. 613/237–3657, fax 613/521–0805). **Australian Federation of Travel Agents** (Level 3, 309 Pitt St., Sydney 2000, Australia, tel. 02/9264–3299, fax 02/9264–1085, www.afta.com.au). **Travel Agents' Association of New Zealand** (Box 1888, Wellington 10033, New Zealand, tel. 04/499–0104, fax 04/499–0827).

TRAVEL AGENCIES

American Express (V, Deák Ferenc u. 10, tel. 1/235–4330, fax 1/267–2028). **Getz International** (V, Falk Miksa u. 5, tel. 1/312–0645 or 1/312–0649, fax 1/312–1014). **Vista Travel Center** (VI, Andrássy út 1, tel. 1/269–6032 or 1/269–6033, fax 1/269–6031).

Visitor Information

➤ IN BUDAPEST: **Budapest Tourist** (I, Déli pályaudvar [South Railway Station]), tel. 1/212–4625 or 1/355–7167; XIII, pedestrian underpass at Nyugati páaudvar [West Railway Station], tel. 1/332–6565). **IBUSZ** (central branch: V, Ferenciek tere 10, tel. 1/485–2700). **TRIBUS Hotel Service** (V, Apáczai Csere János u. 1, tel. 1/318–5776, fax 1/317–9099), open 24 hours. **Tourinform** (V, Sütő u. 2, tel. 1/317–9800). The **Tourism Office of Budapest** (V, Március 15 tér 7, tel. 1/266–0479; VI, Nyugati pályaudvar, tel. 1/302–8580) has developed the **Budapest Card,** which entitles holders to unlimited travel on public transportation; free admission to many museums and sights; and discounts on various services from participating businesses. The cost (at press time) is 2,800 Ft. for two days, 3,400 Ft. for three days; one card is valid for an adult plus one child under 14.

IN THE UNITED STATES AND CANADA: **Hungarian National Tourist Office** (150 E. 58th St., New York, NY 10155, tel. 212/355–0240, fax 212/207–4103). In Canada: **Hungarian Consulate General Office** (121 Bloor St. E, Suite 1115, Toronto M4W3M5, Ontario, tel. 416/923–8981, fax 416/923–2732). In the United Kingdom: **Hungarian National Tourist Board** (c/o Embassy of the Republic of Hungary, Commercial Section, 46 Eaton Pl., London, SW1X 8AL, tel. 0171/823–1032 or 0171/823–1055, fax 0171/823–1459).

➤ **U.S. GOVERNMENT ADVISORIES: U.S. Department of State** (Overseas Citizens Services Office, Room 4811 N.S., 2201 C St. NW, Washington, DC 20520, tel. 202/647–5225 for interactive hot line, 301/946–4400 for computer bulletin board, fax 202/647–3000 for interactive hot line); enclose with inquiries a self-addressed, stamped, business-size envelope.

Web Sites

Do check out the World Wide Web when you're planning. You'll find everything from current weather forecasts to virtual tours of famous cities. Fodor's Web site, www.fodors.com, is a great place to start your on-line travels.

➤ **SUGGESTED WEB SITE: Live Budapest** (www.livebudapest.com).

When to Go

The tourist season generally runs from April or May through October; spring and fall combine good weather with a more bearable level of tourism. Budapest is beautiful year-round, but avoid midsummer (especially July and August) and the Christmas and Easter holidays, when the city is choked with visitors.

CLIMATE

FORECASTS: Weather Channel Connection (tel. 900/932–8437), 95¢ per minute from a Touch-Tone phone.

Average daily maximum and minimum temperatures for Budapest:

Jan.	34F	1C	May	72F	22C	Sept.	73F	23C
	25	– 4		52	11		54	12
Feb.	39F	4C	June	79F	26C	Oct.	61F	16C
	28	– 2		59	15		45	7
Mar.	50F	10C	July	82F	28C	Nov.	46F	8C
	36	2		61	16		37	3
Apr.	63F	17C	Aug.	81F	27C	Dec.	39F	4C
	25	– 4		61	16		30	– 1

HUNGARIAN VOCABULARY

English	Hungarian	Pronunciation

Common Greetings

English	Hungarian	Pronunciation
Hello (good day).	Jó napot./Jó napot kivánok.	**yoh** nuh-poht/**yoh** nuh-poht kee-vah-nohk
Good-bye.	Viszontlátásra.	**vee**-sohnt-lah-tahsh-ruh
Hello/Good-bye (informal).	Szervusz.	**ser**-voos
Good morning.	Jó reggelt kivánok.	**yoh** reg-gelt kee-vah-nohk
Good evening.	Jó estét kivánok.	**yoh** esh-tayt kee-vah-nohk
Ma'am	Asszonyom	**uhs**-sohn-yohm
Miss	Kisasszony	**keesh**-uhs-sohny
Mr./Sir	Uram	**oor**-uhm

To address someone as Mrs., add the suffix "né" to the last name. Mrs. Kovács is then "Kovácsné." To address someone as Mr., use the word "úr" after the last name. Mr. Kovács is then "Kovács úr."

English	Hungarian	Pronunciation
Good morning, Mrs. Kovács/ Mr. Kovács	Jó reggelt, Kovácsné/ Kovács úr.	**yoh** reg-gelt **koh**-vahch-nay/ **koh**-vahch oor
How are you?	Hogy van?	**hohdge** vuhn
Fine, thanks. And you?	Jól vagyok, köszönöm. És maga?	**yohl** vuhdge-ohk **ku(r)**-su(r)-nu(r)m aysh **muh**-guh
What is your name?	Hogy hívják?	**hohdge heev**-yahk
What is your name (informal)?	Hogy hívnak?	**hohdge heev**-nuhk
My name is . . .	(Name) vagyok.	**vuhdge**-ohk
Good luck!	Jó szerencsét!	**yoh** se-ren-chayt

This material is adapted from Living Language™ Fast & Easy Hungarian (Crown Publishers, Inc.). Fast & Easy "survival" courses are available in 15 different languages, including Czech, Hungarian, Polish, and Russian. Each interactive 60-minute cassette teaches more than 300 essential phrases for travelers. Available in bookstores or call 800/733–3000 to order.

Polite Expressions

Please	Kérem szépen	kay-rem **say**-pen
Thank you.	Köszönöm.	**ku(r)**-su(r)-nu(r)m
Thank you very much.	Nagyon szépen köszönöm.	**nuhdge**-ohn **say**-pen **ku(r)**-su(r)-nu(r)m
You're welcome.	Kérem szépen.	kay-rem **say**-pen
You're welcome (informal).	Szivesen.	**see**-vesh-en
Yes, thank you.	Igen, köszönöm.	**ee**-gen **ku(r)**-su(r)-nu(r)m
No, thank you.	Nem, köszönöm.	**nem ku(r)**-su(r)-nu(r)m
Pardon me.	Bocsánat./Elnézést kerek.	**boh**-chah-nuht/**el**-nay-zaysht **kay**-rek
I'm sorry (sympathy, regret).	Sajnálom.	**shuhy**-nahl-ohm
I don't understand.	Nem értem.	nem **ayr**-tem
I don't speak Hungarian very well.	Nem beszélek jól magyarul.	nem **bess**-ayl-ek yohl **muh**-dgeuhr-ool
Do you speak English?	Beszél angolul?	be-sayl **uhn**-gohl-ool
Yes/No	Igen/Nem	**ee**-gen/nem
Speak slowly, please.	Kérem, beszéljen lassan.	kay-rem **bess**-ay-yen **luhsh**-shuhn
Repeat, please.	Ismételje meg, kérem.	**eesh**-may-tel-ye meg **kay**-rem
I don't know.	Nem tudom.	**nem** too-dohm

| Here you are (when giving something). | Tessék. | **tesh**-shayk |
| Excuse me (what did you say)? | Tessék? | **tesh**-shayk |

Directions

Where	Hol	hohl
Excuse me, where is the . . . ?	Elnézést, hol van a . . . ?	**el**-nay-zaysht **hohl** vuhn uh
Excuse me, where is Castle Hill?	Elnézést, hol van a vár?	**el**-nay-zaysht **hohl** vuhn uh **vahr**
Where is the toilet?	Hol van a WC?	**hohl** vuhn uh **vay**-tsay
Where is the bus stop?	Hol van a buszmegálló?	**hohl** vuhn uh **booss**-meg-ahl-loh
Where is the subway station?	Hol van a metró?	**hohl** vuhn uh **met**-roh
Go	Menjen	**men**-yen
To the right	Jobbra	**yohb**-bruh
To the left	Balra	**buhl**-ruh
Straight ahead	Egyenessen előre	**edge**-en-esh-shen e-lu(r)-re
At the end of the street	Az utca végén	uhz **oot**-suh **vay**-gayn
The first left	Az első balra	uhz **el**-shu(r) **buhl**-ruh
Near	Közel	**ku(r)z**-el
It's near here.	Közel van ide.	**ku(r)z**-el vuhn ee-de
Turn	Forduljon	**fohr**-dool-yohn
Go back.	Menjen vissza.	**men**-yen **vees**-suh
Next to . . .	. . . mellett	. . . **mel**-lett

At the Hotel

| Room | Szoba | **soh**-buh |
| I would like a room. | Kérek egy szobát. | **kay**-rek edge **soh**-baht |

For one person	Egy személyre	edge sem-ay-re
For two people	Két személyre	kayt sem-ay-re
For how many nights?	Hány éjszakára?	hahny-suhk-ah-ruh
For tonight	Ma éjszakára	muh ay-suhk-ah-ruh
For two nights	Két éjszakára	kayt ay-suhk-ah-ruh
For a week	Egy hétre	edge hayt-re
Do you have a different room?	Van egy másik szoba?	vuhn edge mahsh-eek soh-buh
With a bath	Fürdőszobával	fewr-du(r)-soh-bah-vuhl
With a shower	Zuhanyal	zoo-huhn-yuhl
With a toilet	WC-vel	vay-tsay vel
The key, please.	Kérem a kulcsot.	kay-rem uh koolch-oht
How much is it?	Mennyibe kerül?	men-yee-be ker-ewl
My bill, please.	Kérem a számlát.	kay-rem uh sahm-laht

At the Restaurant

Café	Kávéház	kah-vay-hahz
Restaurant	Étterem	ayt-ter-rem
Where is a good restaurant?	Hol van egy jó étterem?	hohl vuhn edge yoh ayt-ter-rem
Reservation	Rezerváció	re-zer-vah-tsee-oh
Table for two	Asztal két személyre	uhss-tuhl kayt sem-ay-re
Waiter	Pincér	peen-sayr
Waitress	Pincérnő	peen-sayr-nu(r)

(Waiters and waitresses are more likely to respond to the request "Legyen szíves" [ledge-en-see-vesh], which means "please.")

| I would like the menu, please. | Kérem az étlapot. | kay-rem uhz ayt-luhp-oht |

The wine list, please.	Kérem a borlapot.	**kay**-rem uh **bohr**-luhp oht
Appetizers	Előételek	**el**-u(r)-ay-tel-ek
Main course	Főétel	**fu(r)**-ay-tel
Dessert	Deszert	**dess**-ert
What would you like to drink?	Mit tetszik inni?	meet **tet**-seek **een**-nee
A beer, please.	Egy sört kérek.	edge shurt **kay**-rek
Wine, please.	Bort kérek.	**bohrt kay**-rek
The specialty of the day	A mai ajánlat	uh **muh**-ee **uhy**-ahn-luht
What would you like?	Mit tetszik parancsolni?	meet **tet**-seek **puh**-ruhn-chohl-nee
Can you recommend a good wine?	Tudna ajánlani egy finom bort?	**tood**-nuh **uhy**-ahn-luhn-ee edge **fee**-nohm bohrt
I didn't order this.	Ezt nem rendeltem.	ezt **nem** **ren**-del-tem
The check, please.	Kérem szépen a számlát.	**kay**-rem **say**-pen uh **sahm**-laht
Is the tip included?	Benne van a borravalló?	**ben**-ne vuhn uh **bohr**-ruh-vuhl-loh

Numbers

0	Nulla	**nool**-luh
1	Egy	edge
2	Kettő	**ket**-tu(r)
3	Három	**hah**-rohm
4	Négy	naydge
5	Öt	u(r)t
6	Hat	huht
7	Hét	hayt
8	Nyolc	nyohlts
9	Kilenc	**kee**-lents
10	Tíz	teez
11	Tizenegy	**teez**-en-edge

12	Tizenkettő	**teezen**-ket-tu(r)
13	Tizenhárom	**teez**-en-hah-rohm
14	Tizennégy	**teez**-en-naydge
15	Tizenöt	**teez**-en-u(r)t
16	Tizenhat	**teez**-en-huht
17	Tizenhét	**teez**-en-hayt
18	Tizennyolc	**teez**-en-nyohlts
19	Tizenkilenc	**teez**-en-kee-lents
20	Húsz	hooss
21	Huszonegy	**hooss**-ohn-edge
22	Huszonkettő	**hooss**-ohn-ket-tu(r)
30	Harminc	**huhr**-meents
40	Negyven	**nedge**-ven
50	Ötven	**u(r)t**-ven
60	Hatvan	**huht**-vuhn
70	Hetven	**het**-ven
80	Nyolcvan	**nyohlts**-vuhn
90	Kilencven	**kee**-lents-ven
100	Száz	sahz
1,000	Ezer	e-zer

Days of the Week

Monday	Hétfő	**hayt**-fu(r)
Tuesday	Kedd	ked
Wednesday	Szerda	**ser**-duh
Thursday	Csütörtök	**chew**-tur-tu(r)k
Friday	Péntek	**payn**-tek
Saturday	Szombat	**sohm**-buht
Sunday	Vasárnap	**vuh**-shahr-nuhp

Shopping

Money	Pénz	paynz
Where is the bank?	Hol van a bank?	hohl vohn uh **buhnk**
I would like to change some money.	Szeretnék pénzt beváltani.	**Se**-ret-nayk paynzt **be**-vahl-tuh-nee

Please write it down	Kérem írja fel.	kay-rem eer-yuh fel
How can I help you?	Tessék parancsolni?	tesh-shayk puh-ruhn-chohl-nee
I would like this.	Ezt kérem.	ezt kay-rem
Here it is.	Tessék itt van.	tesh-shayk eet vuhn
Would you care for anything else?	Más valamit?	mahsh vuh-luh-meet
That's all, thanks.	Mást nem kérek, köszönöm.	mahsht nem kay-rek ku(r)-su(r)-nu(r)m
Would you accept a traveler's check?	Elfogadják az utazási csekket?	el-foh-guhd-yahk uhz oot-uhz-ahsh-ee chek-ket
Credit card?	Hitelkártya?	hee-tel-kahr-tyuh
How much?	Mennyi?	men-nyee
Department store	Áruház	ah-roo-hahz
Bakery	Pékség	payk-shayg
Pastry shop	Cukrászda	tsook-rahz-duh
Grocery store	Élelmiszerbolt	ayl-el-mees-er-bohlt
Butcher's shop	Hentes	hen-tesh
I would like a loaf of bread.	Kérek egy kenyeret.	kay-rek edge ke-nyer-et
Bottle of white wine	Üveg fehérbor	ew-veg fe-hayr-bohr
I would like 30 dekagrams of cheese.	Kérek harminc deka sajtot.	kay-rek huhr-meents de-kuh shuhy-toht
Give me six apples.	Tessék adni hat almát.	tesh-shayk uhd-nee huht uhl-maht
Clothing	Ruha	roo-huh
Woman's clothing	Nőiruha	nu(r)-ee-roo-huh
Toys and gifts	Játék és ajándék	yah-tayk aysh uh-yahn-dayk

| Folk art and embroideries | Népművészet és kézimunka | **nayp**-mew-vays-et aysh **kay**-zee-moon-kuh |

The Train Station

I would like a ticket, please.	Egy jegyet kérek.	edge **yedge**-et **kay**-rek
A return ticket	Egy retur jegy	edge **re**-toor yedge
First class	Első osztályú	**el**-shu(r) **ohs**-tahy-oo
Do you have a timetable?	Van itt menetrend?	vuhn eet **me**-net-rend
Is there a dining car?	Van étkezőkocsi?	vuhn **ayt**-kez-u(r)-koh-chee
Sleeping car	Hálókocsi	**hah**-loh-koh-chee
Where is this train going?	Hova megy ez a vonat?	**hoh**-vuh medge ez uh **voh**-nuht
When does the train leave for Pécs?	Mikor indul a vonat Pécsre?	**mee**-kohr **een**-dool uh **voh**-nuht **paych**-re
When does the train arrive from Pécs?	Mikor érkezik a vonat Pécsröl?	**mee**-kohr **ayr**-kez-eek uh **voh**-nuht **paych**-ru(r)l
The train is late.	A vonat késik.	uh **voh**-nuht **kay**-sheek
Can you help me, please?	Tudna segíteni?	**tood**-nuh **she**-geet-e-nee
Can you tell me . . . ?	Meg tudna mondani . . . ?	**meg** tood-nuh **mohn**-duh-nee
I've lost my bags.	Elvesztettem a csomagjaimat.	**el**-ves-tet-tem uh **choh**-muhg-yuh-ee-muht

MENU GUIDE

Getting Started

waiter/waitress	pincér/pincérnő
menu	étlap
wine list	borlap
beverage list	itallap
without meat	hústalan
breakfast	reggeli
lunch	ebéd
supper	vacsora
cup/saucer	csésze/tányér
appetizers	előételek
soups	levesek
salads	saláták
vegetables	köretek
fish	halak
poultry	szárnyas
game	vadas
meat	hús
dessert	deszert
sweets	édességek
fruit	gyümölcs
beverages	italok

Breakfast

bread	kenyér
roll	zsemle
butter	vaj
jam/jelly	lekvár
warm/hot	meleg/forró
cold	hideg
milk	tej
fruit juice	gyümölcslé
eggs	tojások

hard-boiled egg	keménytojás
soft-boiled egg	lágytojás
scrambled eggs	rántotta
ham	sonka
bacon	szalonna
lemon	citrom
sugar	cukor

Appetizers, Snacks, Side Dishes

fruit salad	gyümölcs saláta
cucumber salad	uborka saláta
cheese	sajt
potatoes	burgonya
french fries	sült krumpli
rice	rízs
red cabbage	vöröskáposzta
sandwich	szendvics
Hungarian salami	téliszalami
sausage	kolbasz
frankfurter	vírsli
Hungarian biscuits	pogácsa
fried dough	lángos
cheese-filled Hungarian crepes	túróspalacsinta

Soups

bean soup	bableves
goulash soup (beef stew)	gulyásleves
cold cherry soup	meggyleves
fish stew with paprika	halászlé

Vegetables

cauliflower	karfiol
string beans	zöldbabfőzelék
potatoes	krumpli
onion	hagyma
spinach	spenót

mushroom	gomba
cabbage	káposzta
corn	kukorica
cucumber	uborka
tomato	paradicsom
stuffed cabbage	töltöttkáposzta
potato casserole	rakottkrumpli

Fish

carp	ponty
local fish	fogas
catfish	harcsa

Poultry

chicken	csirke
turkey	pulyka
duck	kacsa
goose	liba
goose liver	libamáj

Meat

veal	borjú
beef	marhahús
lamb	bárány
ham	sonka
pork	sertéshús
breaded meat	rántotthús
chicken paprika	paprikáscsirke
steak	rostélyos

Desserts, Fruit

sweets	édesség
ice cream	fagylalt
whipped cream	tejszínhab
cake	torta
Hungarian crepes	palacsinta

strudel	rétes
chestnut cream	gesztenyecrém
chocolate	csokoládé
walnuts	dió
apple	alma
orange	narancs
pear	körte
sour cherries	meggy
apricot	barack
melon	dinye
layer cake with hardened, caramelized top	dobostorta

Beverages

bottle	üveg
glass	pohár
cup	csésze
beer	sör
wine	bor
white wine	fehér bor
red wine	vörös bor
brandy	pálinka
apricot brandy	barackpálinka
vodka	vodka
lemonade	limonadé
water	víz
mineral water	ásványvíz
soft drink	üditő
ice cubes	jég kockák
coffee	kávé
tea	téa
caffeine free	koffein-mentes

INDEX

FODOR'S POCKET BUDAPEST

EDITORS: Nuha Ansari, Bonnie Bills, Matt Lombardi, Julie Tomasz

EDITORIAL CONTRIBUTORS: Eleanore Boyse, Martha Lagace, Betsy Maury, Paul Olchváry, Robert Rigney, Kristin Rimington, Helayne Schiff, Julie Tomasz, Annie Ward

EDITORIAL PRODUCTION: Stacey Kulig

MAPS: David Lindroth, *cartographer;* Bob Blake and Rebecca Baer, *map editors*

DESIGN: Fabrizio La Rocca, *creative director;* Tigist Getachew, *art director;* Melanie Marin, *photo editor*

PRODUCTION/MANUFACTURING: Yexenia M. Markland

COVER PHOTO Atlantide S.N.C.

COPYRIGHT

Third Edition

ISBN 0–679–00733–4

ISSN 1094–4044

IMPORTANT TIP

Although all prices, opening times, and other details in this book are based on information supplied to us at press time, changes occur all the time in the travel world, and Fodor's cannot accept responsibility for facts that become outdated or for inadvertent errors or omissions. So **always confirm information when it matters,** especially if you're making a detour to visit a specific place.

SPECIAL SALES

Fodor's Travel Publications are available at special discounts for bulk purchases for sales promotions or premiums. Special editions, including personalized covers, excerpts of existing guides, and corporate imprints, can be created in large quantities for special needs. For more information, contact your local bookseller or write to Special Markets, Fodor's Travel Publications, 280 Park Avenue, New York, NY 10017. Inquiries from Canada should be directed to your local Canadian bookseller or sent to Random House of Canada, Ltd., Marketing Department, 2775 Matheson Boulevard East, Mississauga, Ontario L4W 4P7. Inquiries from the United Kingdom should be sent to Fodor's Travel Publications, 20 Vauxhall Bridge Road, London SW1V 2SA, England.

PRINTED IN THE UNITED STATES OF AMERICA

10 9 8 7 6 5 4 3 2 1